D0598561

APR 2 3 2007

Developi
Integrated Curriculum
Using the
Story Model

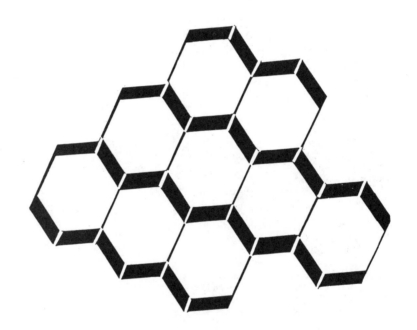

SUSAN M. DRAKE

John Bebbington

Sander Laksman

Pat Mackie

Nancy Maynes

Larry Wayne

Curriculum Series / 64

OISE Press

The Ontario Institute for Studies in Education

The Ontario Institute for Studies in Education has three prime functions: to conduct programs of graduate study in education, to undertake research in education, and to assist in the implementation of the findings of educational studies. The Institute is a college chartered by an Act of the Ontario Legislature in 1965. It is affiliated with the University of Toronto for graduate studies purposes.

The publications program of the Institute has been established to make available information and materials arising from studies in education, to foster the spirit of critical inquiry, and to provide a forum for the exchange of ideas about education. The opinions expressed should be viewed as those of the contributors.

© The Ontario Institute for Studies in Education 1992
252 Bloor Street West
Toronto, Ontario
M5S 1V6

All rights reserved. No part of this publication may be reproduced in any form without permission from the publisher, except for brief passages quoted for review purposes.

Canadian Catalogue in Publication Data

Drake, Susan M., 1944 -
  Developing an integrated curriculum using the story model

(Curriculum Series ; 64)
Includes bibliographical references.
ISBN 0-7744-0394-2

1. Interdisciplinary approach in education.
2. Curriculum planning. 3. Education – Philosophy.
4. Storytelling. I. Title. II. Series: Curriculum
series (Ontario Institute for Studies in Education) ; 64.

LB1025.3.D73 1992   375'.0001   C92-095470-7

ISBN 0-7744-0394-2   Printed in Canada

1 2 3 4 5 6 AP 79 69 59 49 39 29

Contents

Introduction

As we move into the twenty-first century, we are undergoing major challenges. The environment is being destroyed at an ever accelerating rate and the gap between rich and poor widens. Education is also facing major challenges. While knowledge is increasing exponentially, North American students are attacked for knowing less and less. Our present system is not producing the responsible citizen of the future with the life skills to live and work in a global world.

Developing an Integrated Curriculum has been built on the foundations of holistic learning. It has the twofold purpose of encouraging personal growth and empowering students to make positive social change. Holistic curriculum essentially involves making connections. In this book we have worked with interconnections among subject areas, logical and intuitive thinking, mind and body, self and environment. These ideas are expanded upon in *Holistic Curriculum* (Miller, 1988) and *Holistic Learning: A Teacher's Guide to Integrated Studies* (Miller, Cassie, & Drake, 1990). As well, we have focussed on story as a central organizer.

"The Story Model" begins to address the very real concerns of a planet in crisis. We believe that through using some or all of the concepts offered in the following pages, educators can begin to create a "new story" of education. This new story will be about educating the whole person through learning a topic/skill that is meaningful and relevant to the student's life. The new story will acknowledge the values embedded in the educational system – values such as equality for everyone, respect for others, and living in harmony with our environment.

We believe this book can be used in many ways. First, it is a vehicle to develop your curriculum. Second, it identifies the process that many teams will go through to come to a common understanding of integration and a curriculum that comes alive in the classroom.

Explorations as a Curriculum Guideline

We have discovered that the Story Model can be used at many different levels and in many different ways. "Who Am I" and "Local Critters" are two themes that have been explored at the primary/junior level using the Story Model. At this level there is an emphasis on the power of story to connect the child to others and to the world. A webbing strategy that focusses on a real-life setting (this is called a transdisciplinary web in this book and is found on page 22) becomes a planning tool for the teachers. After choosing a topic of interest, teachers can develop activities that are embedded in the real world. Although younger students may not understand words such as technology, law, and economics, they are aware of many daily uses of technology, money, and the police. Setting the curriculum in a real-world context adds meaning and relevance. Also, it illustrates that knowledge is basically interconnected and subject areas are convenient, but not necessarily solid, boundaries by which to make sense of the world.

As students become older and acquire more sophisticated skills, the curriculum allows for greater complexity. Most important is that the topic explored is set in its real-life context. This is done by setting the topic in the transdisciplinary web and exploring the interconnections. Teachers can do this as a guide to curriculum development. Students can do this to gain an understanding of the interconnections and interdependence of all things. Both teachers and students can be involved in planning meaningful and relevant activities.

As we move from the lower grades to the higher ones, "story" remains an important concept. In a recent document, *Rights of Passage* (Hargreaves & Earl, 1990), story has been advocated as a powerful strategy to provide meaning and relevance to students in the transition years. Students are asked to share personal stories that connect them to their topics of interest. In a residential program for grades 7 to 10 on multiculturalism and leadership, students told stories to each other about their culture. Listening skills were emphasized as the stories were told. Students were not only given a voice, but were taught to listen to the voices of others – essentially they learned that we all have a story and this connects us as humans. This increased respect for different cultures. Finally, students were collectively asked to develop a "new story" for Canada, a story where all cultures are honored.

Ideally, this curriculum will be taught in a school without subject area walls. Although education seems to be moving in that direction, it is comforting to know that any teacher can implement some or all of this document within the boundaries of their "speciality." Teachers have found that it often complements existing documents; this seems to be because we tend to think naturally in terms of past/present/future. A grade 10 history class used the concepts of the Story Model and past/present/future to work through a unit on "conflict resolution." The emphasis was on connecting students through story to the human dimension of the topic. Kevin Scull's interpretation of this is available in *Orbit* (May, 1982).

A grade 8 class began a six-week unit on green plants and soil by sharing the life stories of a worm, bee, rain drop, environmentalist, farmer, city dweller, and a scientist working for a chemical company. Students acted in these roles and were interviewed by others. After exploring the topic in a real-life context (with a transdisciplinary web), they generated their own inquiry questions. Ongoing activities included library visits, interviews with people in the community, collecting newspaper articles, and keeping journals. Each student was asked to write a story about a personal connection to plants and the soil and finish with a personal action plan for the future. The selected research question was researched and presented as a play or puppet show. As well, students were asked to design an experiment to explore their question, carry out the experiment, and record the procedure; finally, they evaluated the experiment itself.

A grade 9 geography class spent five weeks exploring "climate" and "trees." During this time, each student adopted and named a tree, wrote a poem dedicated to this tree, made paper, went to a conservation area, visited a newspaper operation, researched many facts about trees that were shared through a collaborative jigsaw, and finally penned their poem on the homemade paper using calligraphy.

In a grade 10 class studying forestry, the focus of "tree" was also used in a five-week block. This gifted class involved English, science, math, and history. These students participated in a simulation game called "Big Lonely." They all became involved members in a logging town dispute in Northern Ontario. Each student assumed a specific character with a specific agenda; they researched the information to play their roles and wore costumes and stayed in character throughout the five weeks. In the end, they voted to allow the town to continue the logging industry in spite of environmentalist demands; the decision came only after profound deliberation based on a wealth of facts researched by the students and presented to the others.

A grade 12 class in Media and English used the model in yet another way. This class used the ongoing daily media to identify the cultural story told by the media and often accepted as truth by the public. Students, whether independently or in groups, followed a topic of personal interest as portrayed by newspapers, movies, and television. The topics ranged from fire, to greenhouse effect, to modelling, to hockey, to disease. Students explored the past, present, and future of their topic and identified the common cultural story and the values embedded in it. Through presentations from each group, a common story emerged and the power of the media to shape our perceptions of the world become frighteningly clear.

At the master of education level, the Story Model was used to teach gender issues and the sociology of education with graduate students. The same principles were used. For example, in the gender issues class, students selected a topic of interest and explored it within the context of the transdisciplinary web. Individual research then prepared the way for presentation through a collaborative jigsaw. Whether students were talking about administration, parenting, nursing, or math and science, the cultural story remains the same. Regardless of situations women have not had a voice or been recognized.

These are a few of the ways that the ideas in this curriculum have been explored. We are delighted by the versatility of the concepts. Better yet, teachers are delighted by the response of most students when invited to pursue a topic of personal interest. We hope other educators will discover a variety of other ways to use this book in curriculum development.

Discovering the Collaborative Process

We have learned that there really can't be a curriculum cookbook for integrated studies. Each team needs to find its own way, its own sense of meaning. This process, as we experienced it, is outlined in Chapter 1. Further research indicates that there is a common process that most teams will go through. We invite you to read this chapter as a guide to the journey ahead.

As the world becomes smaller, and the environment we live in is threatened, there is an increased need for collaboration. We teach our students these skills through either co-operative or collaborative learning. As educators, however, we have had little opportunity to practise this skill. Developing integrated curriculum with a team offers this opportunity. It will be hard work, for collaboration seems to be always embedded with conflict. However, only through collaboration may we develop a "new story" to live and teach by.

There may be many concepts in this book that seem somewhat foreign. Yet, if other educators are like us, they will be pleased at the richness and complexity possible with this curriculum. Teaching from the Story Model perspective has been a growth experience for all of us. It requires an openness of the mind, a willingness to tread unknown territory, and the continual motivation to seek and make the interconnections that are around us. Good luck on the journey ahead!

Susan M. Drake

1
Building an Integrated Curriculum: The Story of Our Process*

We are three men and three women selected from across the province to develop integrated curriculum funded by the Ontario Superintendents' Curriculum Cooperative. Each of us had an expertise in a different subject area and had previous experience with curriculum design. The mandate for this curriculum was that it was to extend the ideas in *Holistic Learning: A Teacher's Guide to Integrated Studies* (Miller, Cassie, & Drake, 1990). Specifically, we would be focussing on the storytelling approach presented in this book. As well, we would be emphasizing a holistic approach to education.

On looking back over the nine days we spent together, it became clear that we had actually undergone a process. We believe that this process is important and may act as a guide for others who choose to take this route in curriculum design. The following is a description of the experience as we interpret it in retrospect.

Letting Go of Old Models
It was clear from the beginning that we were in new territory. We all seemed to hold a slightly different philosophy of education; the first task was to come to a common vision. We spent three days in an orientation process where we were introduced to holistic learning and storytelling.

We used the vehicle of storytelling to accomplish our task of coming to a common understanding. Each person came to the first session with a personal narrative of how he or she had come to be on the curriculum team. Next, we each embedded our personal stories in the journey of the hero/heroine that was offered in Miller, Cassie, and Drake (1990).

We became a cohesive group almost immediately. Members described this sense of cohesion as the freedom to try out new ideas without fear of censure. Each person said he or she had never been in a group that had come together so quickly. Perhaps this was because of a singularity of the group; after some discussion, we found we believed that it was the storying that facilitated this positive working condition.

The power of storying became very meaningful to us personally. It was partially this personal experience that helped us to decide that our curriculum would use story as our starting point. We found that it was stories that connected us. Trusting our own experience, we used the vehicle of storytelling during the rest of curriculum building. For example, we came to the second set of meetings with written stories of our individual "visions." In this way, we all could get an

---

* Reprinted with permission of the Association for Supervision and Curriculum Development.
Note: Some of this section appears in the article, "How Our Team Dissolved the Boundaries," *Educational Leadership* (Drake, 1991).

understanding of what each other was thinking, and still use storying rather than the traditional written set of goals and objectives.

Each of us had a different background in curriculum design. Some had strong leanings toward curriculum that was broken down into small manageable parts, and had a procedural base. Others were more comfortable with a more global approach, where we anticipated the user would gain an overview of the concepts involved and adapt them for classroom use. However, none of us had served on a committee where everyone came from a widely different background, and our commonality was not a subject area but, rather, storytelling. As we moved toward trying to find a suitable framework, there were obvious divisions on format. We spent long hours discussing "hows" and "whys" and what each of us could live with as acceptable.

The only thing that seemed clear was that what we had once understood as curriculum design would not work for this project. We had to let go of old models. It was a realization that we would have again and again. We were aware that letting go of the familiar can be a painful process. And we found that, again and again, when we individually came to a place on the journey where we couldn't find meaning, we would revert back to the way that we knew best. At times these would seem like stumbling blocks; in hindsight, we identified it as a necessary part of the process. Each of us was travelling at a different speed and even that personal speed would vary on different days.

What was most important was that each person could come to personal meaning at every stage of curriculum design. This could take vast amounts of time and sometimes would seem frustrating as we went over and over the same issues and would continually reinterpret what was being presented. As often as not we would end up at the starting point; but not before each of us had wrestled with the concepts until they became meaningful.

Dissolving the Boundaries

If we had to characterize the curriculum process in one phrase the best way to describe it would be the "dissolving of the boundaries." In looking back it seems that each had brought boundaries to this project. In retrospect, and facilitated by the curriculum experience itself, we believe that the boundaries were artificial and existed because of the way we have been taught to view the world. When we began to trust our own experience we found that the boundaries dissolved in many different areas. The following describes some of these areas.

Theory or Practice?

Without a map to follow, and a tendency to fall back into old ways of doing things, we had to remind ourselves constantly to check our own intuitions. Theory aside, how could we best teach what we wanted to teach? Based on our experiences in teaching in general and the theory of holistic learning specifically, we wondered what would work. We struggled with a dialectical process between theory and practice. We believe that our final product is informed by theory/practice and that we can no longer distinguish between the two.

This theory/practice experience could perhaps best be illustrated by our struggle with objectives and evaluation. We knew that all curriculum should start with aims and objectives. Yet we were very hard pressed to be explicit with our objectives. We could not see our way clearly enough to outline the cognitive, affective, and skill objectives that our theoretical upbringing had led us to believe were necessary. We all had a general vision of where we wanted to go. This vision was provided in the stories we had shared with each other on the second set of meetings. As well, we generated a visual picture of the story model during our second set of meetings. Intuitively, we proceeded with building on the visual. We were affirmed when one member read in Egan's *Teaching as Storytelling* (1986) that those who use storytelling as a framework will not be able to isolate objectives. Later, we realized that our cognitive/affective/skill objectives could not be separated because they were embedded in almost every strategy. Holistic learning involves the mind, heart, and body. Our objectives, as found in this document, are more global in nature and are dictated by the elements of storytelling (past, present, future).

When we struggled with evaluation we underwent much the same process. We recognized that the "old story" of evaluation would not fit this storytelling model. Yet, we were caught in a dilemma between the current interpretations of accountability and the goals of our curriculum. We evaluated different documents to see how others had done it before us. However, these did not provide enough answers. How could we effectively measure constructs such as personal meaning, ability to make connections, value shifts, and positive actions? Again we turned to exploring our own "wisdom" as educators. Going back to our own storytelling model, we worked toward developing an evaluation strategy that was in keeping with our holistic objectives. The evaluation as it is presented here is a result of a process with which we are all still wrestling.

Multidisciplinary/Interdisciplinary/Transdisciplinary?

The following diagrams represent the process we went through in developing this model. We were not aware of this continuum when we started and felt relief when it was identified for us midway through the process. These are terms that are identified in *Holistic Learning: A Teacher's Guide to Integrated Studies* and are familiar to people who work within areas that cross disciplines. Once again our experience was validated by theory.

The Multidisciplinary Experience

As we began the experience of building curriculum we believed that we should be able to identify the subject areas that were involved in each teaching strategy. This would allow any teacher to pick up the document and see where he or she fit in. We ourselves represented English, history, geography, science, graphic arts, intermediate grades (special education), physical and health education, and environmental studies. We found that when we worked on a theme, we could easily see the place for "our" subject area. However, we had to squeeze in areas with which we were not familiar; for example, we had a difficult time including math. Yet when a math teacher was involved, the natural place of math in the content was obvious; we had been limited by our own narrow vision. It seems that we started this project looking at curriculum building through the lens of our own area of expertise but began to see how content from other areas could fit into this framework. We later saw this as a "multidisciplinary" approach.

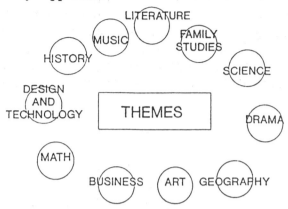

Content is included in several disciplines.

The Interdisciplinary Experience

As we became more comfortable with the concepts of holistic learning and actually got down to sharing strategies for a theme, we found that there was less separation among subject areas than we had previously believed. Content belonged together because there were natural connections. These connections existed because of the theme being explored, rather than because of some intrinsic nature of discrete subject areas. At this point we carefully labelled each activity, breaking it down into the subjects involved. This seemed very important at the time; we wanted to make the document user-friendly and accessible to all. That we often had to struggle to break down an activity into different areas did not seem as important as the fact that we could do it. We later saw this as our "interdisciplinary" stage. Common essential learnings were the foci that connected subject areas.

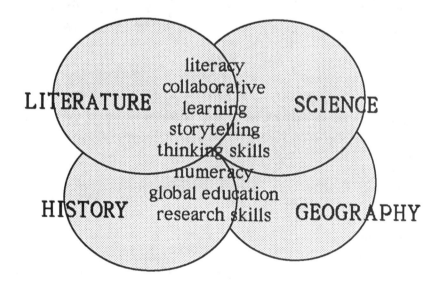

Disciplines overlap in some areas (for example, thinking skills), but each discipline remains discrete.

The Transdisciplinary Experience

After we had been working with curriculum for several days we began to see the futility of breaking things down into their smallest parts. The content and the theme were one and the same. There were no real divisions into subject areas unless we made them. This stage we labelled "transdisciplinary." At this point we abandoned the labelling of subject areas. That is, we erased the divisions we had created up until this point and let the activities stand by themselves. However, it is important to note that we did not do this until we had worked for several days on this project.

No division of disciplines is distinct or perceivable.

We believe that the experience we have described above is a natural progression that most people will have to go through when working on "collaborative interdisciplinary curriculum design." The more experience one has working with others of different expertise, the wider one's focus becomes. As our lenses became wider we could see more and more of the natural connections across the curricula. Eventually we may become "connection experts" rather than subject experts! Each stage requires a shift in perspective and each stage is valuable. The important objective of all perspectives is being able to make connections, a skill which is addressed in this document as a learning outcome for both teacher and student.

Fitting the Curriculum Guidelines

In letting go of old models we also had to let go of certain assumptions that we had all accepted as "truths." The first concern we had was how to fit what we were doing with the demands of Ministry documents and board objectives for skills to be acquired by certain grade levels. We considered trying to take a theme and manipulating it to cover required course content. It did not take long to realize the impossibility of this task. Given that we were producing this for large school boards in Ontario, there was no way we could cover mandates from individual boards and Ministry documents from across all the subject areas.

However, the real reason we could not fit content to previously determined demands was because we discovered that the theme dictated what the content was. We could not manipulate the content to fit a linear framework of knowledge acquisition that we perceived many curriculum documents followed.

How could we be certain that the content was appropriate for the transition years? We found the answer lay within the process itself. We believe that the process is generic in nature. You cannot change the knowledge component of a theme simply because you are teaching it at a different grade level. Instead, we think that this process can be applied to levels ranging from grade 2 to grade 9 to adult education. It is not the content that will change, but rather the sophistication with which one tackles the theme. Given the concept of the student as researcher, the grade 2 student will presumably tackle a theme with less complexity than the older, more sophisticated student. We had to let go of knowledge as being sequential and linear.

Strategy or Content?

Another question that emerged was whether there was a difference between strategy and content. We found that we were often using the arts as strategies to teach facts. For example, we believed that the scientific aspects of a theme could be incorporated into story form and that techniques borrowed from art, drama, or poetry were appropriate ways of demonstrating what had been learned. When did art, drama, or poetry in itself become the focus of teaching? Again the answer seems to be dictated by the content of the theme itself coupled with the expertise of the teacher. We found, for example, that a teacher trained in art could find ample places within any theme where specifics about art technique had a natural place. It was our limitations that put boundaries on possibilities.

We believe that the subject areas that are not given full acknowledgement in this document are a result of the gaps in the curriculum team's knowledge base and experience, rather than that the subject does not have a proper place. For example, we recognized that music was being sadly ignored. To rectify the situation, we briefly explained the storytelling model to a music expert. He presented us with a variety of creative ideas that he believed were intrinsic to our theme (the car) and to storytelling. We could all see the connections he brought to us. However, when we went back to our task, we were hard-pressed to add a rich musical dimension.

As teachers become more familiar with working collaboratively and seeing the world from a transdisciplinary perspective, this inability to see the immediate value of all subject areas will probably change. Meanwhile, we would recommend that as many different subject areas as possible be involved in curriculum building. It may seem to be time-consuming, but this helps everyone to begin to see and think in terms of interconnections.

A primary grade teacher can easily see how curriculum built on a theme is viable. He or she works in this realm every day. However, as we move to higher levels in the school system we are introduced to rotary timetabling and different "subjects." By high school, teachers are identified with and are specialists in the "disciplines." Can this curriculum be taught before there is a complete restructuring of schools?

We believe that this curriculum can be taught in many ways. Because of the current knowledge explosion, teachers cannot continue to add to the required curriculum. Instead, a teacher will have to subtract. This subtraction makes sense if we look at knowledge as it really is, rather than as being divided into artificial categories. We believe that by examining themes we can see what is. Based on our experience, our assumption is that knowledge is indeed transdisciplinary and only by working toward this view can we begin to appreciate it. (If individuals wonder about the artificial categories, they might ask the school librarian how they would go about placing books on the shelves without the help of an arbitrary categorizing system!)

Subject Specialists?

The subject teacher can teach curriculum in his or her area. The lessons will probably take on a multidisciplinary flavor. This teacher can look at a theme that is traditionally linked to his or her area. For example, the history teacher may want to look at Confederation. Utilizing the framework of story, the teacher will examine the past, present, and future. It should quickly become apparent to teachers and students that much more than history is involved; history by its very nature is story which includes politics, economics, and social issues.

Teams of Teachers?

Two or more teachers can team teach the curriculum. We know a geography teacher and an English teacher who are working together on teaching the unit offered in this document. They are teaching it in separate classrooms to the same students. Other teachers may wish to combine classes and have more than one teacher in the room. This teaching will probably involve an interdisciplinary approach. It sets the stage for a real understanding of the transdisciplinary nature of knowledge and is an exciting beginning for the collaboration process.

Transdisciplinary Teacher(s)?

Another approach is for one teacher to teach this curriculum as a "subject" in itself. This would be the transdisciplinary approach. Accustomed as we are to thinking from the lens of our expertise this may appear to be an uncomfortable option for many. However, we believe that the more a teacher works in this tradition, the clearer the interconnections become. This is based on our personal experiences and the shifts we all made during the process itself. Given that the student is researcher, the teacher is not required to have all the facts at his or her fingertips. What is required is the skill of finding information and connecting it. In essence it is learning how to learn in a generic sense.

2
The Story Model

The Story Model is generic. We have chosen one topic (the car within a broader theme of technology) and developed it for the transition years. We believe that the process works for any topic at any educational level. It is essentially a model for understanding the process of change.

The basic premise of the Story Model is that we make meaning by telling stories. Humans for all of recorded time have told stories. We believe that students will come to develop meaning and understanding by exploring their own personal stories and the stories of others.

The Story Model utilizes the concept of story in three major ways:

- as a method for curriculum delivery
- as a metaphor for personal meaning
- as a vehicle for social change

As a Method for Curriculum Delivery

Curriculum can be approached as storytelling. This concept has been well examined in Kieran Egan's *Teaching as Storytelling* (1986). For example, Egan suggests that history is full of stories and science can also be taught as a story. He suggests connecting the cognitive to the affective by telling stories that are more like a newspaper account than a fictional one. This involves working with facts and content from a story perspective.

In every story there is a skeletal framework which involves theme, characters, setting, plot, and resolution. The characters may be objects or animals, but we can relate to them in story form. Students then can put content into the abstract framework of the story; it is a framework that they know well and that is one of the world's most powerful and persuasive ways of communicating meaning. Of central importance is the conflict in the story. Egan suggests that conflict comes in the form of binary opposites. We have chosen to look at how opposing values generate the conflict in our personal and cultural stories.

As a Metaphor for Personal Meaning

We make meaning in our lives through story. Our interpretation of the present is influenced by the way in which we perceive the past and how we anticipate the future. Woven throughout our personal stories are our values and beliefs. In the stories we tell about our lives, the same elements of character, plot, setting, theme, and resolution exist as in any story. As we change and grow, we reinterpret our stories. The events of the past remain the same, but we see them differently. The anticipated future also changes. As well, our values and beliefs evolve.

Change and personal growth are never easy but we are living in an age when we are being confronted with ever-accelerating change from the outside world. Being able to cope with change is becoming a necessary life skill for survival. We, the writers, believe a way to begin to acquire this skill is through consciously working with our personal stories and narratives.

We need to explore why we behave the way we do and decide if we wish to continue with this behavior. This understanding can come from exploring our explicit and implicit values. Our explicit values are the things we say we believe. Our implicit values are often hidden from even ourselves and may be revealed in the things we do. When we act in ways that contradict our explicit values, we are exposing our real values and belief system. For example, a person may say, "I believe in loving other people." However, when that person cultivates friendships because of what he or she can gain, the implicit or hidden value is to get ahead rather than develop loving relationships.

Our personal stories are influenced by important people from the past, by life experiences, and by the "cultural story" in which we live. Chapter 2 of *Holistic Learning: A Teacher's Guide to Integrated Studies* (Miller, Cassie, & Drake, 1990) provides a deeper understanding of personal story.

As a Vehicle for Social Change

All of our personal stories are set in, and profoundly influenced by, our cultural story. The cultural story is the way we story our culture; that is, the way we talk about ourselves and our society, the lens from which we view our world. It is so much a part of us that we often don't question it; the values and beliefs embedded in this larger story have become our assumptions of reality. However, if we were living in a different culture, such as Chinese or African, we would hold different beliefs about reality and therefore act in different ways.

Our modern version of the North American cultural story is set in the advent of the Information Age. Many of us are still living in the Industrial Age but are being swept forward into a new story by technological advances that impact on almost every aspect of our lives. The cultural story is told to us by such institutions as schools, churches, and governments. It is reinforced by the powerful media. It is a story of progress and unlimited growth in the land of opportunity. It is a story where the individual can thrive through entrepreneurial activity.

Like the personal story, the cultural story is accompanied by values and beliefs which evolve as the story changes. As we have moved from the industrial story to the information story, our values and beliefs have changed. For example, technology is highly valued for making our lives easier and facilitating a high standard of living. Yet, in many ways we live in a society where technology is controlling us. As we become numbers in a large system, we lose the value of human connection. Technology itself is value-free. It is a tool of the people who develop it. The values assigned to technology are embedded within our cultural story.

As in the personal story, we need to examine the explicit and implicit values of our culture. We say we value equality for all; yet our legal system and schools are set up to perpetuate the *status quo*, a *status quo* where there are not yet equal opportunities for visible minorities or women.

Experiencing Time in a Story Model

This model begins with a focus and revolves around the story behind the focus. As in all stories there is a past, present, and future. We begin with the present and look back to interpreting the past, then forward to an anticipated future before we collaboratively develop a new story. It is important to note that there will probably be issues with temporality as students work with this model. The categorization of time into past, present, and future will blur. Often it is difficult to tell what time period one actually is considering. For example, students come to identify negative aspects of the present story as "old story" and positive aspects as "new story." We have found this experience is a characteristic of working with story itself. As we move forward with this curriculum, students will hopefully be learning and growing. This in itself will guarantee that the past, present, and future will become intertwined. It is helpful for students to understand this concept of time for they will certainly experience it; yet, it is also necessary to freeze time and create a collective "perceived past" and "anticipated future" in order to work with this framework.

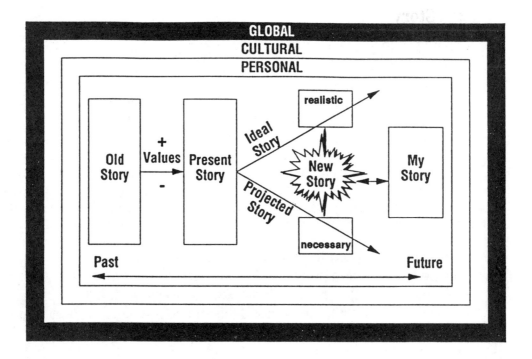

1. Identify why the present story is in a "state of flux" or change.
2. Identify the roots of the conflict by looking at the past or old story. Identify the explicit and implicit values in the old story.
3. Explore the future through:
   - the projected story (if we continue to act according to the implicit values of the old story);
   - the ideal story, which can be developed by examining alternative views of the future proposed by such groups as environmentalists, Greenpeace, futurists, feminists, and holistic educators. Elicit the values inherent in these emerging stories.
4. Create a new story by integrating the <u>realistic</u> from the ideal story and the <u>necessary</u> from the projected story.
5. Develop a personal action plan which will facilitate the new story becoming reality.
   - These steps have been adapted from Feinstein and Krippner's *Personal Mythology* (1988).

Please Note: In all stages of identifying the story, the personal narrative of the student is intended to be connected to the cultural narrative.

The Model Applied to "The Car"

Present Story

The first step involves examining the current story using the focus of "the car." When a transdisciplinary focus is used, the story becomes global (see transdisciplinary webs in "Key Holistic Learning Strategies" on page 22). For example, the car is really an international vehicle when viewed from the perspective of the natural resources and computer expertise required to construct it. Many of the resources needed to fuel the current-day car come from the Middle East which has led to an uneasy political situation globally. The car is essential to the North American economy for the jobs it provides and the efficient transportation it offers. The car is a symbol of the North American way of life: prestige, freedom, and independence are its calling card. However, we are living in an age of unprecedented change. The current story no longer works. For example, the car, despite its advantages, is the major polluter on a planet whose survival is at stake.

Old Story (Perceived Past)

Students need to understand why the current story is no longer working. To understand this fully, we need to explore the roots of the conflict by looking at the old story. Again, this is done through a transdisciplinary focus. This involves exploring the history of the car as a god of the Industrial Age. People left their rural communities to live in urban centres and work at jobs on a line in an industrial factory. The car offered people a freedom and ease of transportation they had never known. The world became much smaller and goods could be brought in from long distances. The wealthy could parade their wealth with fancy cars; the poor used public transportation. Still everyone seemed better off for this vehicle of convenience. How is the perceived past affecting the current story? The values and beliefs embedded in the old story are still with us today and strongly influence our actions. Through this exploration students will probably discover a society where the explicit values are independence, autonomy, achievement, equality, and caring for fellow humans. When they look for the implicit values (revealed by actions rather than words), they may find a value system dominated by power, achievement, materialism, autonomy, and greed. It is these values that are still with us in the present story, some of which threaten to destroy the planet.

New Story (The Anticipated Future)

The Projected Story

Students are asked to imagine what life will be like by the year 2030 if we continue to live as we do. This suggests that if we continue to behave in ways consistent with the value system whose roots are in the "old story," the planet will not survive. For example, if we continue to allow the car to dominate our lives, we will be suffocated by the pollution caused by the automobile itself.

The Ideal Story

There is an ideal scenario that could be constructed for the year 2030. Today there are several "emerging stories" which tell us how we should live to survive. Students might consider the opinions of groups such as the environmentalists, Greenpeace, futurists, Amnesty International, or feminists for their visions as examples of an ideal story. When they examine the explicit values behind these stories, they will probably find a respect for all life on the planet, an acknowledgement of the interconnectedness of all things, and a willingness to live in harmony with the planet. It is a story grounded in values of love, co-operation, and compassion. They are the same explicit values as in the "old story." The difference, students may comment, is that the explicit values will have to be acted upon, rather than simply spoken, in order to survive.

Creating a New Story

This stage involves two basic steps: (1) deciding what is realistic to expect from the emerging ideal scenarios; and (2) choosing what is essential to keep from the "old story."

Realistically, the ideal scenarios of the future cannot be actualized. Human nature will probably never allow people to live in total harmony. Conflict is a part of any story, be it cultural or personal. However, if our personal stories are embedded in a new cultural story that has different values, we may be able to change behavior at personal and social levels. This new story should incorporate the vision of harmony on the planet, equality, respect for others, and an understanding of the interconnectedness of all things. On the other hand, students must wrestle with the essential elements that we would like to keep for a good standard of living. For example, we may feel we need to keep the efficient transportation system offered by the car.

Students should become aware that the creation of a "new story" involves a real dilemma. It seems we cannot have the positive without the negative. In focussing on the car, it appears that an efficient transportation system allowing for independence is not possible without paying the price of pollution. These types of dilemmas arise regardless of the focus being pursued.

Students can collaborate to create a "new story." This new story in its turn acts as a central core story to guide their actions. Because the beliefs and values in this story have presumably evolved since the old story, it is hoped this new story will enable and empower people to act in different ways.

A practical example of a "new story" is provided in the environmental actions in our schools today. Young people recycle paper as a matter of course. It is a part of the cultural story they live by (in contrast to many adults still living by the old story of consumerism). It is a story promoted by schools and the media. The value of conservation is rapidly becoming internalized.

Action

This last step requires connecting the cultural and personal story. What is the student going to do to begin to make the new story a reality? This stage involves personal exploration into the perceived past, present, and anticipated future. By what values does the student live? Are these the values that he or she wants to continue to hold?

Armed with a set of explicit values, the student can set goals to make these a reality. Creative problem solving can offer new solutions to old dilemmas. The personal story has been embedded in a new cultural story. This stage asks for a personal commitment.

Story Model as a Generic Approach

We believe that the Story Model is generic and can be used with any focus area of interest. We have found that it is best to concentrate on a specific focus and then expand the focus to explore a wider theme. In our experience, we discovered that if we tried to use a broad theme we would get lost in the process. Here are some ideas that have been tried and tested. Have fun discovering your own.

Theme (General)	Focus (Concrete Example)
Nature	trees
	loons
	dogs
	green plants
	bears
Relationships	gender issues
	friendship
	body language
	native peoples
Government	The Constitution
	war
Health	food
	nurses
	drugs
	aging population

Values Embedded in the "New Story"

We are not dictating what the "new story" should be; we expect students to create such a story collaboratively. However, we are promoting certain values for the new story which can be found in *Values, Influences and Peers* (1984) and are consistent with the world's great religions. These values are:

comparison	patience
co-operation	peace
courage	respect for life
courtesy	respect for others
freedom	respect for self
generosity	responsibility
honesty	self-discipline
justice	sensitivity
loyalty	tolerance
moderation	

From a global perspective we value the equality of all people, the interdependence of all things, respect for the planet, and living in harmony and balance.

3
Beginning the Journey

As curriculum designers, we believe that teachers are the best judges of how to present material to their classes. We know that teachers choose and adapt to best suit their needs. For this reason we are offering a generic package that we believe teachers can modify according to their situational contexts, students, and programs. We believe that this curriculum is easily accessible to all teachers and will help them to move toward a more holistic approach to instruction. The curriculum has been designed to allow teachers to build on their own intuitions about good teaching. The activities can be modified to adapt to the needs of the students and the comfort levels of teachers.

We believe that the teacher who is moving toward a holistic philosophy:

- has a profound belief in human potential;
- believes in educating the whole person in relation to his or her social, ecological, political, and economic contexts;
- sees learning as a lifelong process;
- recognizes a range of learning styles and tailors teaching strategies to differing needs;
- believes that learning should be personally relevant and should provide meaning and purpose to the students' lives;
- provides strategies for intuitive knowing as well as linear thinking processes;
- acknowledges and values multiple intelligences such as interpersonal, spatial, musical, artistic, language, and mathematical intelligences (Howard Gardner, *Frames of Mind*, 1983);
- is aware of his or her own inner life and is always in the process of personal growth;
- recognizes the power of the teacher as a role model in the classroom;
- is willing to risk being authentic;
- is globally minded and promotes harmony on the planet through both talk and personal action; and
- knows with certainty that he or she can make a difference!

We believe that such a teacher will enjoy using this document.

As the last rays of afternoon sunlight streamed in the windows, Ms Green surveyed the students in her classroom intent upon the task in front of them. She smiled to herself, delighted by the way the theme "The Car and Technology" had been received by her grade 9 students. When she used storytelling as pedagogy, the theme seemed to come alive. At first she had been skeptical both of her own ability to tell a good story and that storytelling had the power to connect the essential content across different "disciplines." How needless her worries had been. She had discovered that the historical stories of technological advances had been a fascinating study in itself. Storytelling came naturally once she had risked teaching this way and had begun to search out the stories behind the facts.

She had focussed on the automobile as an entry point. Stories about legendary characters such as Mr Ford followed the pattern of mythological heroes across different cultures and connected people from ancient times to modern times. The effect of the technology of the car was changing the environment in irreversible ways and these stories were researched by her students and presented as dramas in the classroom. She had especially liked the one where the group had created a tragic drama where the key characters Land, Air, and Natural Resources battled out their conflict with Car itself. Examining new technologies had led the class into speculations about the design of the future car and future transportation systems. Other serious questions arose, such as how to train people to be able to work in an automobile industry where the technology is changing so quickly that there is no way to teach skills with the technology that will exist when the students get to the workplace. Interviews that the students had conducted at local businesses and organizations indicated that keeping up with new technologies is a universal problem in modern society. Students wrestled with the question of what should be taught in school. Should we be learning technical skills or should we be learning how to learn?

They also became aware of a world view where technology designed to control our environment was possibly controlling us. Although technology offers more predictability, often it is at the expense of humanity; production lines in the manufacturing plant attest to this phenomenon. The car which was to increase our quality of life by liberating us, in many ways actually restricts us. For example, if you don't have a driver's licence, you don't have recognized identification.

Students also realized that technology has a way of increasing the stratification in society. Stories were told of how low bridges built on the New York State Parkways in the '30s allowed access only to private cars and restricted the buses which were ridden by the poor and predominantly African Americans. Students unearthed many stories of how we are dominated by technology in the industrialized nations. Horror stories were told of Third World countries where inappropriate technologies have been imported from supposedly well-meaning richer nations. The never-ending need for oil to fuel the car and its political implications had the class investigating the role of the military in a global economy. Perhaps most frightening of all was the role the car plays in destroying our environment.

As Ms Green reviewed the path of the students' learning journey, she realized that indeed some very real concerns had been raised about technology and humanity. Each student had reflected on his or her own life in context of the discussions. How had they followed the same path as the heroes who invented the car? How had their lives been influenced by technology, be it the computer or the car? How would their lives be influenced in the future if the car remained the symbol of freedom and power for North Americans? What were their own value systems? What could they do about what they didn't like? Already several students had begun to ride their bicycles to school and others were taking the bus and arranging car pools. To Ms Green this was a clear indicator that the unit had meaning for her students.

The feedback from parents was also heartening. Students came home and discussed issues from class with their families. They had become deeply involved and, as a result, well-informed. They were aware that the real impact of technology was not acknowledged in their home lives. The learning was definitely continuing outside the classroom. Family members were finding that their own behavior was shifting as they became more aware of technology and its impact on the environment and the very quality of life.

The students were happy with learning this way. For them, the connections among subject areas were so apparent it was hard to believe that there were distinct disciplines which claimed certain knowledge as unique to their spheres. The stories were interesting, and they found that it was especially meaningful to narrate their own stories, whether they were from their personal life experiences or from how certain things had occurred on the planet. The reflections had been done in storytelling style through journals, group sharing, role playing, and group storywriting. They liked combining the arts with learning. It was fun connecting art, music, and drama to make stories come alive. They liked learning strategies such as guided imagery where they could create mental pictures of events either factual or imaginary; they found they remembered much better this way. The exploratory field trips showed them that the things they were learning were really about living a life full of meaning and purpose, not just some dry old facts.

Ms. Green had excelled at establishing an inviting learning environment. Students knew that it was okay to try things such as drawing or singing. These were areas where they had previously lacked confidence. They knew now that there were more facets to intelligence than getting good marks in math and literature. They were fascinated by the things that now assumed meaning for them because they had been put in the context of their own lives. They had learned how to be researchers rather than receivers of knowledge. They became aware of the interconnectedness among all things and how they connected to each other and to all of humanity.

They were learning how to act in ways that were in keeping with a planetary consciousness; this meant in practical terms caring for and nurturing each other and the planet we share. In short, they were beginning to create a "collective new story" to live by in a world that is characterized by flux and transformation. The new story would guide them as they made their way through the crises that are an inevitable consequence of being human. The curriculum was a curriculum with heart.

T's Journey

We expect that the teacher who chooses to implement this curriculum will be exploring some new territory and this means that there is a personal journey ahead. It is a journey that requires an educator who accepts change as a challenge and as a vehicle to personal growth. He or she understands that change, by its nature, involves endings (loss), a struggle (anxiety) before the reward (joy). It is a journey where the teacher will meet his or her own demons and dragons along the way. It Is a journey that requires courage and belief in oneself; for the natural tendency is to resist the unknown or to turn back when the going gets tough. A story of the teacher's journey is included in the narratives in the Appendix. It is called T's Journey.

4
Key Holistic Learning Strategies

Holistic learning is a teaching and learning process that recognizes that people learn in different ways, which can include the visual, auditory, and kinesthetic modes, and recognizes the affective, cognitive, and physical domains. Holistic learning acknowledges Howard Gardner's multiple intelligences (*Frames of Mind*, 1983) and also views interpersonal, intrapersonal, musical, artistic, and spatial intelligences as important to develop.

Holistic teaching techniques focus on making the holistic approach to learning relevant and meaningful for the students. Such strategies facilitate making connections between mind and body; self and inner self, self and environment; subject areas; logical thinking and intuitive thinking. Curriculum that is designed for holistic learning includes not only the body, mind, and spirit but the head, hands, and heart.

Holistic learning strategies that we have focussed on in this document include:

- transdisciplinary (real-world) webs
- student as researcher
- storytelling
    power of story
    initiating the storytelling
    students and storying
    responding to stories
    drama
    exploring values in stories
- visualization
- metaphor
- journal writing

Transdisciplinary (Real-World) Webs

The concept of "transdisciplinary webs" emerged during our experimentation with the Story Model. It is a key learning strategy for this work and transcends the disciplines to set the topic in a real life context. This strategy will facilitate the following outcomes:

- It will allow students to experience the interconnections across the disciplines.
- It will establish an entry point for the student as a self-directed researcher.
- It will begin to develop the cultural story based on the "facts" generated by the transdisciplinary webs.
- It will allow for the exploration of the implicit values that are inherent in the cultural story.

Transdisciplinary webs can be understood by comparing them to semantic webbing. Teachers may be familiar with semantic webbing which is traditionally used in curriculum building centred on themes. The topic of focus is placed in the middle of the page (for example, car) and a circle is drawn around it. Different ideas and connections that are associated with the focus are then connected by drawing spokes to the central idea and writing down a key word to represent the information. An example of semantic webbing would be:

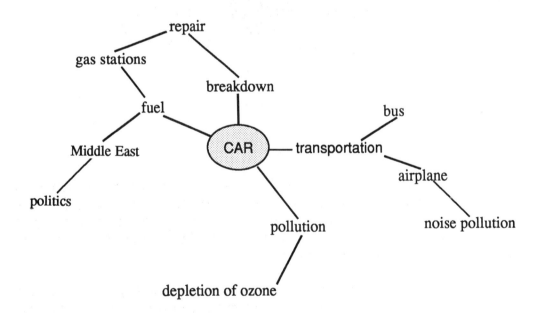

We have found that semantic webbing is a somewhat linear approach that does not facilitate a full understanding of interconnections. Although semantic webbing is an excellent tool to work with story, we found that when we wished to work from a global perspective we needed to go beyond this to "transdisciplinary webbing."

That is, we would brainstorm as many facts as we knew about a car as set in a real-world context; then, we would include each "discipline" in our brainstorming rather than use a free association process. This procedure differs from semantic webbing in that the free association of ideas is directed through a real-life lens. Usually the traditional school subjects–English history, geography, science, math, health, and physical education are already included in a real-world context. Art, drama, and music may be an integral part of the focus or may be utilized as strategies by which one can teach the curriculum. Religion adds a rich element to whatever focus is chosen. It is extremely important to begin with technology, economics (business), politics (law), media, social issues, environment, and global view. It is only by inclusion of these concepts that students will arrive at the richest picture of our "cultural" story.

We found the following procedure helpful:

1. Put focus (for example, car) in the centre of the page in block letters.

2. The trigger words politics (law), economics (business), technology, media, global view, environment, and social issues are circled in an inner circle around the focus, leaving room for free associations of ideas.

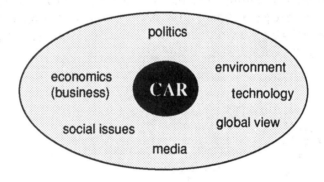

Real World Web

3. An outer circle is created by writing down the words of the traditional disciplines such as language arts, history, mathematics, geography, science, health, drama, music, literature, art, and physical education. Art, music, and drama may be part of the process of generating the content in the web or they may be used as strategies to connect and elaborate upon the content.

4. Brainstorm for ideas or concepts that you already know. Begin by generating ideas in the inner circle then move to the outer circle to expand ideas. Then fill in the outer circle by brainstorming for the known. Don't be concerned when you find that a fact under one heading could also be written under another one. This is part of the process.

5. Use lines (webs) to show interconnections among ideas.

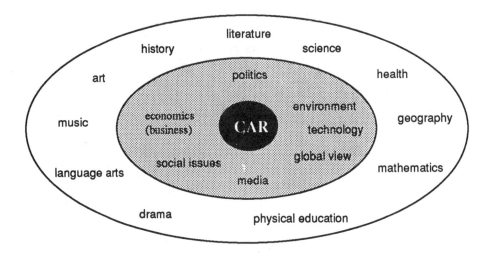

Transdisciplinary Web

We have seen transdisciplinary webs being used with foci from:
- body language (communication theme);
- trees (environment);
- gender issues, friendship (relationships);
- native peoples, constitution, war (government);
- Easter (celebrations), dogs, loons (animal kingdom);
- food, nurses, drugs, aging populations (health sciences); and
- female adult learners (education).

In each case the focus was a specific concrete example within a more general theme.

We found that when the focus was developed with a transdisciplinary point of view, the same big picture emerged. It was the "old story" of our culture. When people engage in this process they begin to see interconnections among disciplines.

For example, using the focus of the car people begin by brainstorming the inner or real-world circle of the transdisciplinary web. To understand interconnections enter one door of the inner circle and choose a salient fact. Then, see how this salient aspect affects or is affected by other areas on the inner circle. For example, when entering the technology door, people often select car design. As they reflect on car design they see how this impacts other areas of the inner circle. It might look as follows: The desire for new car designs is promoted by the media and this results in keeping jobs in the work force. Politicians are concerned that people have jobs and also that they are re-elected. To stay in power they usually require periods of economic stability. Laws are passed which increase safety, such as seat belts, and reduce pollution, such as requiring unleaded gas. Yet a problem still exists from an environmental perspective. Increasingly, there are health problems found by the depletion of the ozone layer which is linked to the car. To address the problems with cars will cost dollars and jobs and this may lose the politician the popular vote. As well, not everyone in North America can afford cars, thus driving home social inequalities. These inequalities become more pronounced when the car is examined from a global perspective. Most people in the Third World, for example, cannot afford to have a car. Yet, it seems that everyone wants a car or the means to an efficient transportation system.

The experience is much like looking into a kaleidoscope. When you look into it you see a pattern of interconnections. Turn the kaleidoscope and the pieces shift to create an entirely new pattern. Wherever you start the transdisciplinary web, you create one pattern of interconnected facts. Approach the topic from another avenue and you have a different pattern of exactly the same parts. This sense of interconnectedness is reinforced when students draw other transdisciplinary webs using different foci.

We believe that both teacher and students should experience a transdisciplinary web near the beginning of any unit in this storytelling approach. The teacher (or teachers) needs to create the web to understand the complexities of the focus and how best to develop curriculum from it. The students need to create the webs themselves with their current knowledge base. This creation serves two purposes: (1) it facilitates making connections; and (2) it is only after the web has been created that students can generate a rich list of questions that they may then research.

There is one note of caution here. Students need to produce as much content as they can from their current knowledge base before generating the research questions. We found that if the questions were asked first, rather than fully brainstorming, the questions stopped the process of developing an ever-enlarging and ever-connecting knowledge base.

Clearly, this webbing strategy is more suitable for older than younger students. However, grades 5 and 6 students are certainly capable of understanding and creating the web when the trigger words (for example, technology, social issues) are explained to them in a context they understand. Primary/junior teachers have used the web to plan activities set in a real-world context. As well, it teaches younger students about connections rather than fragmenting knowledge into subject areas.

Student as Researcher

A key concept of the curriculum is that the student is a self-directed researcher. A fundamental premise is that students need to find personal meaning in the topic under investigation. This means that the student should be answering questions that are personally relevant.

Transdisciplinary webbing is a significant stage in the development of the student as researcher. After creating the web, students become aware of the vast range of approaches from which they can inquire about the car. Students are asked to generate their own questions and then to answer them through independent research.

MALASPINA UNIVERSITY-COLLEGE LIBRARY

In practice, we have found that the student as researcher can involve solitary independent inquiry or a more collaborative process. A group of students may wish to explore one aspect of the story (past, present, and future) such as the design of the car. Other groups may choose to examine aspects affecting the car such as economic impact, vehicular laws, media influence, or environmental impact. Some available research resources are:

- library archives
- folk songs
- photographs
- old newspapers
- diaries
- travelogues

- historical accounts
- oral histories
- interviews
- films
- videos
- field trips

Research can be presented in traditional style (for example, written report) or using one of the more innovative story strategies presented in this book. In essence, each individual or collaborative group will have researched a piece of a very large jigsaw or one particular perspective of the kaleidoscope. During the presentations, a great deal of overlapping of content will become apparent. At first, students may be uncomfortable and think that other students or groups have "stolen" their ideas. This is a wonderful opportunity for the teacher to explore the reality of the interconnections.

Storytelling

The Power of Story

"The drive to story is basic in all human beings. Stories shape our lives and our culture — we cannot live without them." (Barton & Booth, 1990)

Stories, whether personal or cultural, have the power not only to entertain but to transform us. They help us to deepen our awareness and understanding of ourselves and our relationships to each other, our heritages, and the world in which we live.

We tell stories in order to make sense and meaning of our lives and experiences. It is the vehicle through which we integrate new knowledge and become aware of the ancient wisdom that resides in our hearts. We tell and retell our lives as stories to ourselves and to others, and in so doing, our personal narratives become explicit. By reflecting on these stories, we achieve greater levels of self-awareness and understanding that allow us to move forward with our lives.

The extensive use of story and storying in the classroom meets the needs of students on many levels. As an art form, storying is an effective strategy for developing and educating the imagination. Story addresses the whole child — intellectually, emotionally, and through dramatic exploration, physically. Story gives validity to our students' feelings and helps them deal constructively with their inner lives. It provides them with direction and the comfort of knowing that their problems are not unique to themselves, but are universal. In responding to story, students are able to test themselves imaginatively and vicariously in lived-through experiences with story protagonists. Embedding personal stories into larger stories can provide students with valuable information, self-confidence, and self-knowledge that can then be applied to their own journeys through life.

It is story that defines a society and binds it together. In exploring the stories of past ages, students develop a heightened sense of what it would have been like to have lived during those times. As past and present stories are directly related, an awareness of past stories illuminates our present cultural, political, and economic situations.

Likewise, our emerging stories will determine our collective future. In working with the activities suggested in this book, students will be actively involved in making the current story explicit and in using this story as a starting point for engaging in the decision-making and value-forming processes that may influence the development of a new story. Through storying activities, students will be empowered to create their own futures and to participate in the development of a new cultural story.

Through practice, students will come to recognize that stories are characterized by embedded values that can be made explicit, thereby enabling the listener to hear at both a literal and an interpretive level.

Initiating the Storytelling

Initially, teachers may be apprehensive about their own abilities to tell stories, and students may also feel this way. We have found that everyone is a natural storyteller. (An assumption of this book is that humans are storytelling animals and that we make meaning by telling stories.) We offer some suggestions to get started which are based on our personal experiences.

- Personal stories are a good starting point. A story that is not personal will be easier to tell if you feel a personal connection to it.
- Write out the story and then let it percolate in your subconscious before telling it.
- Choose a story where you feel a real emotion attached to an experience. Focus on that emotion as you tell the story.
- Practice a story before you tell it. Focus on your emotions and the images the story evokes for you. Feel what is happening in the story.
- Practice in front of a mirror. This is particularly helpful to gain confidence and make the story come alive through appropriate body language and interesting voice intonations.
- Tell the story from your heart.
- Connect to students in your audience. Find appreciative students and tell the story to them. You will recognize them by their wide eyes and nodding heads. Do include everyone by making eye contact across the audience.
- The audience will connect to the emotional content of the story. The emotion is attached to the images of the story. Help students to "see" the picture and relate it to their own past experience. Relate the unknown to known.
- For further suggestions read Bob Barton's (1986) *Tell Me Another*.

Students and Storying

Students may be initially shy or even skeptical about storytelling. After all, stories are for children and they probably haven't had much exposure to such "silly" stuff since childhood. However, it doesn't take long to rediscover the power of storying. In our experience, students will quickly ask "Can I tell a story?" This makes the content personal and relevant. The following suggestions are some ways we have found to encourage storytelling :

1. Choose a topic with which everyone can make a personal connection. For example: Can you remember a significant (or insignificant) experience with a car? a tree? a bicycle? climbing? jumping?

   In pairs, one student tells a story to the other. The second student listens and retells the story. The first student listens to the retelling without interjecting. Reverse the process. Pairs might reflect on how the stories were transformed; what was omitted ...

   Move students into fours and tell these stories; then eights. At this point the teacher can ask students if anyone would share his or her story with the class.

2. Create the setting for a story by giving a guided imagery. Have students relax. Baroque music in the background helps to set the stage. Begin to tell a story such as ...

   You are in the middle of a dark but comforting forest where the sun is shining through the trees and you hear the birds chirping.... Ahead of you is a path through the forest.... Feeling relaxed and comfortable, you move along the path and notice the forest surrounding you, the small animals darting underfoot, the gentle noise of the breezes.... Now you see a light on the horizon and find yourself drawn toward the light.... The forest thins and you find yourself in a wide open meadow filled with flowers.... The light is brighter now and you see it clearly at the top of a mountain which appears in the distance.... You move quickly toward the light...

   The students finish the story in their imagination as the music plays (about three to five minutes). They can then write and/or share their experiences. Murdock's (1987) *Spinning Inward* has many excellent suggestions for this type of activity.

3. The teacher could use a reflective relaxation session to promote further understanding about storytelling. Students are asked to relax, close their eyes, and turn their attention to a series of questions. There should be a pause of thirty to sixty seconds between questions. Some questions could be:

   Who is the storyteller in your family?
   Where/when are stories told?
   Are certain stories told and retold?
   Is a certain family member the central character of many stories?
   Can you recall a family story?
   Are you an important part of the story?
   If you do not think of family conversations as storytelling,
     how would you characterize them?

   Students complete this activity by writing for twenty minutes and then dividing into small groups to share stories and look for commonalities and differences.

4. Each student is asked to choose a story to analyse. This story may be provided by the teacher, or students may choose a favorite story or perhaps a story studied in another class. In focussing on the central character, students reflect on questions such as the following:

What are the personal, social, cultural, and economic forces
affecting the character?
How does the character deal with these forces?
What choices does the character have?

Students are asked to follow the same process with a personal story. The objective of this exercise is for students to understand how their personal stories are a part of the larger cultural story.

* Activities #3 and #4 have been adapted from Wendy Hesford's *Storytelling and the Dynamics of Feminist Teaching* (1990).

Responding to Stories

These activities are designed to help students come to personal meaning and connection. The teacher can select activities according to the level of sophistication of the students as storytellers.

1.   The teacher could have students respond to narratives in the curriculum by:

   • using a round-robin method for retelling the story;
   • retelling the story from another point of view (for example, retell the Blacksmith's story from the point of view of the Blacksmith's apprentice; see the Appendix);
   • writing in role by adopting a story character's persona and rewriting the story from that point of view;
   • retelling the story collaboratively whereby students interpret the story while retelling it. This can be done by creating a readers' theatre where students write a collaborative script with a narrator's part included (for example, a radio play). Another technique is story theatre where one student narrates the story while the others enact it; and
   • having the students respond by generating a list of questions for which they would like to find answers and then developing an activity, an experiment, or a strategy to begin to answer their questions.

2.   The teacher could extend student responses to the narratives by having students engage in any of the following:

   • role playing;
   • creating a comic strip;
   • interviewing (in or out of role);
   • listening to oral histories from local people;
   • choosing or creating a theme song to represent the values of the story;
   • creating a tableaux;
   • creating a story or a dance to represent the values of the story;
   • telling the story through mime (body language only);
   • responding in a journal;
   • art work which simulates mood or tone of the story;
   • graphic representation of relationships; and
   • equations to represent cause and effect.

Drama

Drama is a way of storytelling. Drama strategies promote experiential student-centred learning. It provides opportunities for students to become fully involved in imagining, exploring, enacting, communicating, and reflecting upon ideas, concepts, and feelings. Drama activities are holistic. They encourage students to involve themselves physically, emotionally, and intuitively, as well as intellectually.

Drama strategies such as tableaux and ritual are creative art forms that allow students to focus thought, feeling, and intuition into a single visual image or action. Ritual is repeated collaborative action that illustrates a value of the group. It can be as simple as lighting a candle to mark an important event or it can involve more elaborate preparations to signify transformation. Tableaux is a picture that group(s) of students can create for various purposes. For example, students can freeze a moment of "work" in the car factory.

Dramatic role-play invites students to step imaginatively into the lives of others and explore life situations from other points of view. This can facilitate the development of empathy and a greater understanding of the motivations of others. As well, students' attitudes and values can be illuminated through contrasting them with those of the "others" they role-play. In reflecting on their experiences in role-play, students develop greater degrees of self-awareness that lead to personal growth.

Exploring Values in Stories

Have students consider the conflicting values inherent in the stories that are provided. Students could draw these values on either end of a two-way arrow to make the conflict explicit.

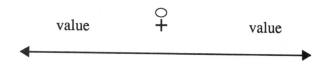

By showing a sketch of a person on the "conflict arrow," students can demonstrate the personal nature of a values conflict.

A physical value line could be used to start a discussion about conflicting values. For a selected issue, the teacher makes a statement that identifies a value position. Explain the concept of a value line to the students. Ask the students where they would fit on the value line in relation to the statement made by the teacher.

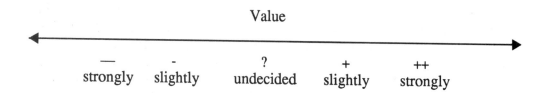

Each person commits to his or her present value system by pinning a sign on the chest with the selected value position pinned on it. Have students pair with someone who has the same view as they do and exchange their reasons for their view. Next, have them find someone who is one position removed from their opinion and meet briefly with that person to exchange views non-critically. Finally, have each student find an individual who is two positions removed from his or her own and once more share viewpoints non-critically. After this is completed have each student write a reaction or response to his or her personal opinion on the issue.

Visualization

Visualization is a picture or image that one sees in the mind. It is often referred to as seeing with the mind's eye. People primarily use the visual sense, but visualization can be auditory, emotional, and muscular. Blind people can visualize using other senses. A student who has trouble visualizing can be asked to reflect on what he or she is hearing or feeling. If a student has trouble seeing pictures, asking for a description of his or her bedroom with closed eyes usually evokes a picture and demonstrates to the student that he or she can visualize. Alternatively, ask a student to visualize tasting a lemon or smelling freshly baked bread. This will quickly illustrate how taste and smell are a part of the imagery process.

Visualization may take the form of a student creating an image of something that he or she may wish to achieve such as doing well in school or performing well in sports. At another level the student may spontaneously experience free associations which can provide personal insights and intuitions. The process of visualization can be self-directed or guided by someone else. Guided imagery occurs when the teacher or a learning partner verbally guides the learner through a visualization experience. Relaxation exercises enhance the experience. Visualizations might be used in the classrooms for distinctly different functions. Four different functions are offered below.

Goal Setting

When a student knows that he or she wishes to achieve a certain goal, it is possible to create a picture of this achievement in the mind's eye. Goals can range from very concrete ones, such as being relaxed and handling a job interview well, to the abstract, such as demonstrating compassion in everyday living. It is important that the imager sees the goal in its ideal form. For example, a basketball player who visualizes scoring baskets should be aware of excellent technique and visualize himself or herself shooting in perfect form. Students then need to be knowledgeable about their "vision" or they will indeed act out what they see. As well, students need to be cautioned about their goal images. The old saying "be careful what you want, you may get it" is very true here. Students need to ask if their goal is positive, realistic, and will not hurt others. At the same time as a goal needs to be realistic, it should also be beyond students' grasp. It is a fine balance. A goal that is too difficult sets someone up for failure. Yet, visualization has the power of allowing students to push past personal limits. Understanding this tension between realism and challenge helps students to find the most suitable goal to visualize. As they achieve one goal, they can then move on to visualizing another one.

Increasing Self-Awareness

Visualizations often offer valuable personal information to the learner whether the process is self- or other-directed. For example, the teacher may lead the student to imagine a wise person (the learner's intuitive self) who has come to give the learner a significant message. The wise person is actually the intuitive or inner self who often possesses inner wisdom to help with problem solving.

When visualization is used to surface and connect thoughts and feelings, it may involve either free associations or verbal guidance from either a learning partner or a teacher. Such a visualization might be used in esteem-building exercises where students are talked through the process of re-examining something that happened to them and recalling how they felt, what they thought, and what meaning they attach to their thoughts and feelings. They can then visualize a different sequence of events to make the past event more positive.

Learning Abstract Ideas and Concepts

When visualization is used to make abstract ideas and concepts clearer, the visualization will be guided. The guide will talk the learner through an idea that will allow the learner to make fuller use of his or her senses, intuitions, and feelings to make personal meaning of the idea. This is particularly useful in teaching scientific or technological concepts. For example, a teacher might create a guided visualization to have students experience a water cycle. In such a visualization, students would imagine themselves as a drop of water being warmed by the sun and evaporating, being cooled, joining with other water droplets, falling, and so on. Visualization can be used in all "subject areas." For example, a visualization where students become the angle in a mathematical construction increases understanding of spatial visualization.

Enhancing Creativity and Intuitive Thinking

Students can be directed to relax and imagine a movie in their mind's eye. For example, a student can fly all over the globe and visit the Amazon forests, an Inuit community, and a large urban city in one session. They can use their imaginations to solve problems creatively that they have witnessed during the visualization.

Metaphor

Teaching with metaphor is a powerful tool in holistic learning. Metaphor can be used at two levels. One, it can increase understanding. Two, it can generate new ways of thinking about things; new ways of problem solving. At first, students will struggle with this new way of learning. Then, in our experience, they will discover that they are natural metaphor-makers. As teachers we need to trust that left to their own devices students will be creative in developing metaphors.

Increase Understanding

Students can develop metaphors to explain existing theories or concepts. For example, students can develop a metaphor to describe the greenhouse effect, pollution in their local backyards, or traffic patterns. This type of metaphor does not generate new knowledge; rather it allows students to sort out the complexities and relationships within an existing framework. Students may work in a group to develop a metaphor and then show it to others. Questions then can be raised which tease out the nuances.

Generative Metaphors

Metaphors which allow us to see problems in a new light tend to generate new ways of knowing and being. For example, the students can compare themselves to the car they are most like in personality. To do this students will need to "become" the car of their choice; this involves attributing to the car particular personality characteristics. This type of exercise facilitates students articulating new aspects of self.

Generative metaphor strategies are particularly useful in problem solving. The student could choose the car which represents what he or she would most like to be. Then, they would make the reasons for their choice explicit. In this way students are articulating their ideal self. Next, they view a problem through the eyes of the "ideal self" and how it would be solved by the "ideal self."

The "Journey of the Hero" (or "The Quest") offers an interesting problem-solving metaphor. The hero (student) is called to adventure. Then he or she must make endings and separate from the familiar world. Next, there is the struggle of confronting the demons and dragons. After the dragon is slain, the hero receives the reward and is joyful. Finally, he or she must return back to the world that was left behind and offer service to others.

As a problem-solving metaphor the hero can expect the following:

Stage	Plan For
Call to Adventure	desire to resist change — confusion, dissonance
Ending	explicit endings, support through feelings of loss
Struggle	anxiety, anguish, making mistakes, support for anxiety, risk-taking
Beginnings	internalization of new identity, celebration/joy
Return	service to others

For further understanding of the quest as a metaphor, read chapter 2 in Miller et al. (1990) or *The Journey of the Learner* (Drake, 1991).

Journal Writing

The value of journals lies in the opportunity for the student to reflect on the personal meaning of what is being learned through the classroom activities. In a personal notebook, students have opportunities to write their thoughts and feelings about previous experiences or to express their concerns about the future.

Journal writing may be either structured or unstructured, read by the teacher or not, commented upon or not. Teachers may provide students with specific questions or ideas to address, or during an unstructured writing opportunity, students are free to focus on the ideas or events that have become a personal highlight. The privacy of a journal may vary with the topic. The many variations will require that teachers who wish to use journals think through the possibilities beforehand and communicate very clearly their purpose and intended practice.

Reflective thinking is often difficult for students to do. One method for getting students to explore further is to use the metaphor of unpeeling the onion layers. Students are asked to explore the first layer of the onion by examining what it is. Further exploration involves moving from "what" and asking questions such as "why?," "so what?," "what does this mean to my life?," "how?," and "now what?" This questioning will probably reveal other layers of the onion and this in turn will indicate that it is time to start the whole process again.

Some students may continue to explore one theme in their journal and peel away the layers over time. Other students may wish to shift from idea to idea. However, it is important that teachers encourage students to reflect, to go beyond what happened on the surface, to explore a deeper reality.

Journal writing provides an excellent opportunity for the teacher to connect with the student in important ways. It is here that the teacher can gain a sense of the student both intellectually and emotionally. A dialogue between teacher and student is possible when the teacher writes a response on a regular basis in the journal. The responses may be supportive and/or challenging; however, this use of journal dialogue is a powerful teaching strategy which facilitates reflective thinking and personalizes the learning.

5
Sample Unit

FOCUS: The Car

THEME: Technology

Adapting the Model for Personal Use

Based on our experiences we offer the following recommendations for adapting the model for personal use:

- Find out existing beliefs and values of curriculum writers as soon as possible. These include beliefs about curriculum writing and what it is important for a student to learn.
- Be ready to let go of old models of curriculum design.
- Decide on a format for writing early in the process. How will you address learning outcomes? evaluation? Does your school or board have a policy? Many groups find it useful to design their own formats.
- Use an organizer to begin the talking. We suggest a transdisciplinary web. Semantic webbing or curriculum mapping (using the outside circle of transdisciplinary web only) is also useful.
- Allow a lot of time for planning (a year seems to be about right). Talking to each other both formally and informally is also important.
- Use volunteer labor only! Begin slowly and let the integration process grow as it makes sense to you.
- Expect conflict. Through conflict comes creativity. Respect individual differences.
- Remember that coming to personal meaning is a most important part of the process. When you encounter a block, experiment in the classroom with the ideas that you are uncomfortable with.
- DEVELOP YOUR OWN TEACHING STRATEGIES COLLABORATIVELY. Use the ideas in this sample unit as a guide only. You will probably discover that developing strategies is the easiest part of the process.
- Choose your own theme and work with the Story Model as it makes sense to you.

We, the writing team, have used this model in a variety of settings and have discovered that it can be used at different levels of complexity. The following scenarios offer some examples of suggested uses:

- The model may be used to examine a topic through the present-day lens only using semantic webbing (p. 22). This is similar to more traditional approaches to integrated curriculum design.
- The present "story" may be examined by exploring the focus from a transdisciplinary web perspective.
- The present "story" may be further enriched by examining the explicit and implicit values that are embedded in the story. Discovering and articulating the values is a challenging activity for learners of all ages. The inner circle of the transdisciplinary web is a good place to begin the search. Behaviors are easy to identify. The question becomes "What values drive these behaviors?"
- The focus may be explored for content from the past, present, and future lens without including the cultural or global aspects of story.

Unit Objectives

Students will have the opportunity to:
- understand the past, present, and anticipated future of the car;
- be able to internalize the information through narrative;
- research factual content from a transdisciplinary perspective;
- make explicit the values that are embedded in the past, present, and anticipated future;
- create a new story, through projection of oneself into a new narrative; and
- start the process of understanding the story model that is used in this document.

Ongoing Unit Activities: Personal Connections

1. Students are instructed to collect articles from newspapers and magazines throughout the unit. Articles may be specifically about the car or may be more generally about technologies. These articles facilitate the highlighting of the current relevancy of this issue and also give it a global perspective. Suggested activities include:
   - An individual scrapbook where the student organizes collected items to "tell" the current story as presented by the print media.
   - A collective bulletin board where the class can discuss the direction of the current story whenever it is relevant to class activities.
   - Students using items in their journal or learning log as triggers for reflection.
   - Each student being responsible for bringing a news item to class for a specific day. General class discussion can follow.
2. Have students keep an ongoing learning log to monitor their progress, needs, and future learning plans. Possible questions might be:
   - "What did you learn?"
   - "What do you want to find out?"
   - "What will you do about it?"

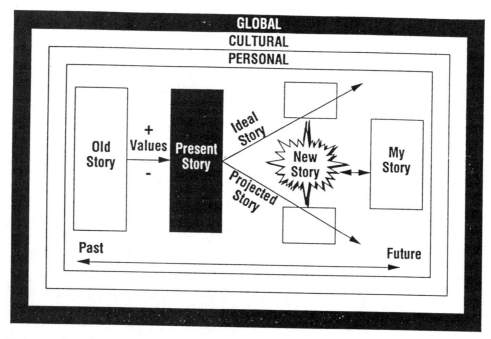

Present Story

The perceived past and anticipated future are a part of the present.

Objective

To identify the Present Story and the values inherent in it.

It is helpful to present students with the entire model near the beginning of the unit. A visual representation left on a bulletin board is very useful to refer to during the course.

Activities #4, #5, #16, and #17 are central to fully developing the Story Model. Once the transdisciplinary web has been created, the students (as researchers) are asked to begin to focus on an aspect of personal interest and to research this aspect. The research process could consider past, present, and future. Research is to be done individually or in groups and presented later to the class. As well, after developing the transdisciplinary web, students can begin to identify the "cultural story" and elicit the implicit and explicit values inherent in it.

Suggested Activities

1. The teacher may introduce the unit by recounting a personal story about an experience with a car. Students are asked to recall a story about a car. A student then relates his or her story to a partner or small group. The teacher could then ask students to work in triads to incorporate the ideas from the separate stories

into a collaborative story to present to the class. Students may choose from a variety of presentation styles; some choices might be role-playing, a dramatic reading, pictures, song, poetry, or pantomime. During these activities, students are asked to note questions that they have about the car. Follow the presentations with discussion questions such as: "Do you think cars are important?" or "In what way is a car important to you?" Students are then encouraged to generate a list of their own questions such as: "What was life like before the car became important?"

2. Ask students to complete the sentences in a questionnaire concerning the role of the car in their lives. Sample sentences could be:

    • A car is important because ...
    • An exciting experience I had in a car ...
    • The car of my dreams is ...
    • The first family car I remember is ...
    • A funny experience I had in a car was ...

    Organize information in a way to illustrate the collective experience of the class, for example, classification chart, diamond ranking.

3. As a starting point, have students ask questions that focus on their individual interests about the car. If students have trouble generating questions, small groups could be formed and each group asked to generate one "what", "when", "why", "where", and "what if" question. Example questions might be provided, such as "What is the experience of breathing at a busy intersection?"

4. Present the class with the Story Model and give an overview of how the model can be interpreted (pp. 9-15). A visual representation of the model posted in the classroom is helpful in allowing students to see the "big picture" while exploring the smaller ones. It also gives them a common vocabulary to discuss the experience.

5. Have students work in groups to create a transdisciplinary web around the focus of the car. The transdisciplinary web is used to develop a global context. For example, the car is really an international vehicle when viewed from the perspective of the natural resources and computer expertise required to construct it. Many of the resources needed to fuel the present-day car come from the Middle East. This has led to an uneasy political situation globally. The car is essential to North American economy for the jobs it provides and the efficient transportation it offers. The car is a symbol of the North American way of life; prestige, freedom, and independence are its calling card.

    To create a transdisciplinary web:

    • Put the focus (for example, cars) in the centre of a page.
    • Include economics, law, politics, media, technology, and social issues as trigger words for inner circle representing the real-world context.
    • Brainstorm ideas and facts related to cars.
    • Draw lines between areas that connect (see model on page 22).
    • Create an outer circle with subject areas as trigger words.
    • Repeat the brainstorming and connection process.

Finally, students select (individually or in a group) one aspect of the transdisciplinary web that they would like to research. This becomes an ongoing activity. The teacher/librarian can be very helpful here. At the end of the unit, students are asked to present their research in an interesting and creative way. Although students are at first apprehensive of this "creativity challenge", we have found that they more than answer this task through art, drama, music, and activities that require group involvement.

6. Have students work in small groups to map out on a large sheet of paper some of the ways that different people in their local environment are dependent on the automobile. This is an "interdependent map"; this idea was suggested in *Global Teacher, Global Learner* (Pike & Shelby, 1988).

7. Have students listen to Thomas Berry's story (Appendix) of his first view of a car through a guided imagery that the teacher directs. Students could then write a journal entry that examines their own family use of the car or discuss Berry's point of view and how it compares to their own. They might also draft a (possible) letter to Thomas Berry to explain their opinions.

8. Have students take a traffic survey at a busy intersection. Several visits could be made over a number of days. Guide students to be sensitive to sights, sounds, and smells. Students could record their observations in a writer's notebook. Using these observations, they could then write poems that describe the experience through metaphor. Following their visit to the intersections, students might create "a soundscape." To do this, they could imagine a trip in a car that travels from the country to the city and suburbs then back out to the country. Students present to their classmates a list of mechanical and voice noises that they heard in each part of the trip (for example, the wail of a hundred out-of-tune orchestras, an army of mechanical ants fighting through a frightening maze). They could also create a "soundscript" to represent the sounds they heard. Instruments could be everyday items and voice.

   Alternatively, students might be directed to make observations that will enable them to respond to the following questions:

   • Which vehicles transported the greatest number in the most efficient manner?
   • Which vehicles appeared to be least polluting? most polluting?
   • How did the drivers of these vehicles relate to each other in the various traffic conditions that you noticed?
   • How did you respond personally to this experience (thoughts, feelings, concerns)?

9. Set up an experiment that will allow students to examine the quality of air coming through a screen or direct vent to the outside. Put a fine layer of vaseline on a cotton ball and hang it at a screen/vent indoors. Examine the surface of the cotton after two or three days. Alternatively, students could design air filters for these vents and try to construct one for use in front of the vent (for example, use common materials like layers of cheese cloth). Students could write a journal entry in response to the question, "What do the results of this experiment mean to me?" These responses could be shared in small groups.

10. Have students take two elastics to examine the effect of pollution on their elasticity. Keep one elastic inside and set another outside, fully exposed. Keep the indoor elastic in a plastic bag so that it is totally protected from the environment. After two weeks, stretch each elastic to examine its elasticity. Repeat this procedure with different thicknesses of elastic bands. Use a forcemeter to measure the elasticity of each elastic band and draw graphs to show the relative forces that can be sustained by each. As in Activity 7, students should have an opportunity to respond to and discuss the results of this experiment. The concept of elasticity or the inability to "stretch" might be developed as a metaphor for the Present Story.

11. Working in pairs, write down as many types of raw materials as you can think of that are part of a working car. Identify where each raw material originated (for example, country, continent, and so on). Repeat this for the components of the car (for example, radios, glass, and so on). These activities should illustrate how the car is truly an "international" entity. Students can research the effects of auto part production on the cultures in which they are made. New learning can be presented through reports, story, or drama.

12. Have students examine several media advertisements for cars and discuss the strategies that are used to make these cars desirable. Students may want to discuss how they feel about these strategies. Students could design an "ad" campaign for an efficient, environmentally friendly car. This might include radio and television commercials.

13. Have students design a machine to demonstrate three forms of energy: heat, light, and motion. Challenge students to think of alternative ways of using the different materials that may be available to transform energy. Teachers might hold an invention convention to display the devices that the students develop. Students could even try to incorporate their devices into alternative ways of generating power for a car. A "media campaign" may be launched to sell these cars to the public.

14. Visit a busy gasoline station and calculate how much gasoline is sold in fifteen minutes. Multiply this by four times the number of hours that the station is open to estimate the daily sales. Multiply by the number of days the station is open each week to estimate weekly sales. Ask the management to provide their average volume sold each week in order to verify findings. Have students compare different stations and develop a pie graph to show the shared information. Pie graphs can be constructed by having the students find the total volume of gasoline used in one week and then calculate the percentage of gasoline sold by each station. To find the number of degrees that this would represent in the pie graph, multiply the percentage by 3.6. Construct a circle and use a protractor to construct the "slices of the pie." The information obtained may be used as part of the "media campaign" suggested in Activity 12.

15. Use activity suggested under "Exploring Values in Stories" on pages 30 and 31.

16. The old story is no longer working. Have students identify the problems with

the old story by examining the problems of the present (for example, a result of the old story is pollution from cars). Ask students to suggest why the present story is not working any longer.

Have students identify both the positive and negative aspects of the present story. From these, have them suggest what aspects they feel are worth keeping and what the cost is to keep them. This could be organized in a chart form:

Negatives	Positives	Valuable	Cost
expensive	convenience	yes no	
	jobs	yes	
	exciting technology		

17. On the posted diagram of the Story Model, have students re-examine and identify the values inherent in the old story and present story.

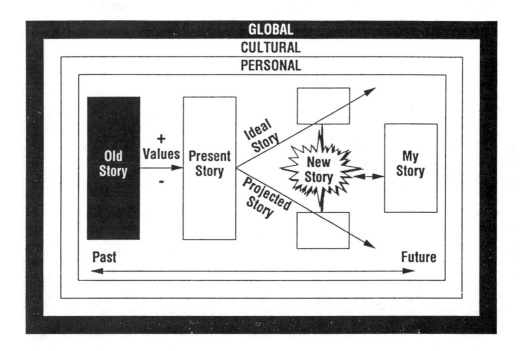

Old Story

The perceived past which has brought us to the present.

Objectives

To identify the old story (past) and the values inherent in it.

Students need to understand why the present story is no longer working. To understand this fully, we need to explore the roots of the conflict by looking at the past story. Again, this is done with a transdisciplinary focus. This involves exploring the history of the car as a god of the Industrial Age. People left their rural communities to live in urban centres and work at jobs on a line in an industrial factory. The car offered people a freedom and ease of transportation they had never known. The world became much smaller and goods could be brought in from long distances. The rich could parade their wealth with fancy cars; the poor used public transportation. Still everyone seemed better off for this vehicle of convenience.

How is the perceived past affecting the present-day story? The values and beliefs embedded in the old story are still with us today and strongly influence our actions. Students will probably discover a society where the explicit values are independence, autonomy, achievement, equality, and caring for fellow humans. When they look for the implicit values revealed by actions rather than words, they may find a value system dominated by power, achievement, materials, autonomy, and greed. It is these values that are still with us in the present story and some of them are threatening to destroy all beings on the planet.

> If the teacher wishes to implement the model to its fullest extent, the perspective of the transdisciplinary web is necessary throughout the examination of the entire unit. Although the web activity does not need to be repeated, it is helpful to refer to it continually to ensure a variety of connections. As well, students should be continuing on with their own research.

Suggested Activities

1. Have students either develop their own story about the car's past or use one of the stories provided in the Appendix. Students should work in pairs to retell the story. In each pair assign an A and B. A's portray a person from the nineteenth century. B's are interviewers from the present day. A's are interviewed by B's. Students should use ideas collected from past activities to inform their roles here.

   Tell A's: *"Think about your role. Who are you? What do you do for a living? What is life like for you? What do you most want your interviewer to know about you? Take a few minutes to jot down your ideas concerning this."*

   Tell B's: *"Work with two or three other B's to generate a list of questions that will elicit greater understanding of life a century ago."* Sample questions might be: *"How did the values of a hundred years ago differ from those of today?"*, *"What was the lifestyle of people at that time?"*, or *"Why did it take so long to get around in the past?"*

   After interviews are completed, each interviewer may introduce his or her interviewee and tell the class what was revealed during the interview.

2. Have students work in groups of five to create a series of three different tableaux which illustrate how people lived in the past. (A tableaux is a frozen picture that students make with their bodies.) Students may present their work theatre-style, or all groups may "perform" their tableaux simultaneously.

3. Have students write a journal entry in-role as a person who lived in their community at the turn of the century. Consider their role at that time, what a normal day consisted of, what their concerns or problems are.
   Have students choose one sentence from their journal entries to read aloud in turn. Use the "collage" of lines to create a "found poem" which can be recorded or displayed. Students can ask "What does our 'poem' tell us about life before the car?"

4. The teacher may use the following narrative as guided imagery to establish the setting for a movement activity:

   "Take a few deep breaths and relax all the parts of your body (relaxation music helps to establish the setting) ... relax your toes ... feet ... ankles ... legs ... buttocks ... stomach ... back ... chest ... shoulders ... neck ... jaw ... cheeks ... eyes ... forehead ... scalp ... brain ....

Imagine that you are a young person who lived about a century ago. You think back to the time you saw your first car. You knew when you saw the first 'horseless carriage' noisily careening past your house that soon your life would be changed forever. Times were tough. ... Most of the townsfolk were unemployed and cheered when the automobile plant on the edge of town began hiring. The town itself could not supply all of the workers that were needed, and hundreds of young men left their farms in the surrounding countryside to try for one of the steady jobs at the plant. Many of them did get work, and soon rows of two-storey houses, all exactly alike, began to sprout up around the plant to house the workers and their families.

Iron and steel were needed to produce cars, and soon the plant owners built a foundry near the plant to supply their needs. Then billows of sooty, noxious gases spewed from the smokestacks day and night, filling the air and covering the town's stately brick homes with layers of grime.

You have gone to work in either the automobile plant or in one of the factories that supply materials for it. You work on an assembly line doing the same monotonous job twelve hours a day, six days a week. The environment in which you work is noisy, dirty, hot, and dangerous. Sparks from the unguarded machinery fly about you and the air is continually filled with grey, sooty smoke. Now slowly and in your own time come back to the here and now."

The teacher can now follow this with a movement activity:
In groups of five, create the assembly line you are working on. See how long you can keep repeating the same movements. Speed it up ... Slow it down to "slow motion." Freeze to create a tableaux.

Teacher wanders around the frozen assembly line, asking questions of individual "workers":

- What is your job in this plant?
- How long have you been working here?
- Do you make enough money to live?
- How do you feel at the moment?
- How is life different for you since the automobile became so important?
- How is it better?
- How is it worse?

5. In early twentieth-century Glasgow, Scotland, it used to take three policemen to apprehend a speeding motorist. One would stand near a lamp post, and as the motorist passed, wave a handkerchief. Another policeman with a stopwatch would start timing the car and stop as it passed by. Since the lamp posts were distanced evenly apart, the second man would check the time against the distance covered from the first man by the motorist. If the motorist was speeding, the second policeman signalled a third policeman who stopped the speeding car.

   Pairs of students could repeat this strategy by measuring the distance between lamp posts and the posted speed limit to calculate the time it would take a car to pass legally between two points. By using a stopwatch and stationing themselves at the beginning and the end of the selected timed run, they could record the progress of a number of cars and then calculate the percentage of speeders versus non-speeders.

   All groups could share their information and all groups could create graphs to show their results. Students could consider reasons for speeding, and the perceived need for cars that can travel considerably faster than the speed limits.

6. Students create two equal-sized drawings or paintings showing a car from the past and a present-day one. Each picture should include a background that shows the effect of the car on the environment. Each picture is cut into equal width strips but is kept in order (for example, two centimeters). These strips are then glued to another piece of paper as long in length as the first two pictures. The strips are alternated in order, and their edges must touch when they are glued down (for example, the first strip of the past, the first strip of the present, and so on). When this is completed, the new picture is folded on the edges of the past/present strips to create a fan. When viewed from different sides, the displayed work will show the aspect of change by changing sides to view from.

7. Have students work in groups of three or four to write a version of the old story with themselves in the story. Share stories with the class either through such activities as dramatic reading or role-playing. Then, from this perspective of the past, have them identify the values in the old story. This is a challenging activity. Students should look at what people said and how they acted. What they say was important will reveal the explicit values. What they actually did will reveal the implicit values.

8. The old story is no longer working. Have students identify the problems with the old story by examining the problems of the present (for example, a result of the old story is pollution from cars). Ask students to suggest why the present story is not working any longer.

   Have students identify both the positive and negative aspects of the present story. From these, have them suggest what aspects they feel are worth keeping and what the cost is to keep them. This could be organized in a chart form:

Negatives	Positives	Valuable	Cost
	convenience	yes	
expensive		no	
	jobs	yes	
	exciting technology		

9. Develop a timeline of values from past to present. Branches could be drawn from the stated values on the timeline and examples and/or effects of this value written down on the branches.

10. On the posted diagram of the Story Model, students continue to identify the values inherent in the old story and present story.

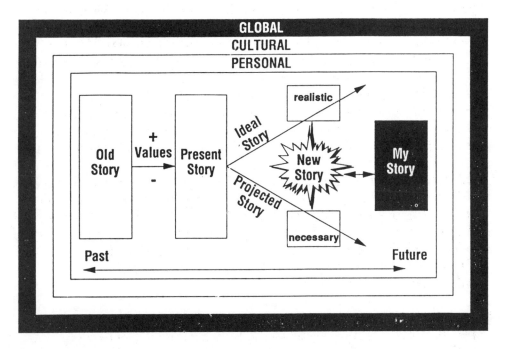

The anticipated future may be the probable story, the ideal story, or a new story that begins to reconcile the probable and the ideal.

Objectives

- To recognize and make explicit the probable story, ideal story, and a new story;
- To discover the values embedded in each story; and
- To create a new story with positive values to guide us.

Probable Story
The future (if we continue to act as we are currently acting).

Ideal Story
The future as an ideal. Versions of this story are emerging in our time from groups such as Greenpeace, Amnesty International, feminists, environmentalists, holistic educators, and futurists.

New Story
A story which realistically combines the useful and the practical from the old story and the positive values of the ideal story. The realism in this story comes from reconciling the negative elements that seem to be inherent in the useful aspects of the old story. For example, the car has provided highly valued individual freedom at a major cost to the environment.

Creating a New Story
This stage involves two basic steps: (1) deciding what is realistic to expect from

the emerging ideal scenarios and (2) choosing what is necessary to keep from the "old story."

Realistically, the ideal scenario of the future can't be actualized. Human nature will probably never allow people to live in total harmony. Conflict is a part of any story, be it cultural or personal. However, if our personal stories are embedded in a new cultural story that has different values, we may be able to change behavior at a personal and social level. This new story should incorporate the vision of harmony on the planet, equality and respect for all, and an understanding of the interconnections among all things. On the other hand, it must wrestle with the necessary elements that we would like to keep.

Students should become aware here that the creation of a "new story" involves a real dilemma. Apparently we can't have the positive without the negative. In focussing on the car, it seems at present we can't have an efficient transportation system allowing for the independence of the population without the price of pollution. These types of dilemmas seem to be involved, regardless of the focus being pursued.

Together, students can collaborate on creating a new story. This new story then acts as a central core story to guide our actions. Because the beliefs and values in this story have presumably evolved since the old story, it is hoped this new story will enable and empower people to act in different ways.

Suggested Activities

1. Have students explore the future from versions provided in futuristic television programs such as "Star Trek: The Next Generation," or from stories by authors such as H.G. Wells or Isaac Asimov. Ask students why films and other media present such bleak views of the future compared to "Star Trek: The Next Generation." Short stories by Raymond Bradbury might motivate students to create their own fantasies. After having examined possible futures, have students generate their personal narratives of the future. These narratives can be used in the same way as they were in the old and present story.

2. Have students examine current print resources such as newspapers for ideas on car-related products. Create a future artifact related to the car. Alternatively, students could create an ensemblage, a 3-D product, to represent the idea of the car but with the person's personal values clearly represented. Students can use "found objects" or clean garbage to create their ensemblage. It is necessary to use an appropriate glue such as fast-drying epoxy glue to join the different materials. An ensemblage usually is free-standing and must be planned and organized so that it can be seen from all sides.

3. To identify the probable story, have students project the world situation to 2010 if current trends continue. They should include descriptions of what will happen from a transdisciplinary perspective (that is, geology, geography, sociology, history, economics, and so on). The values that are implicit in this projected future should be made explicit. Place these values on the Story Model diagram that is posted in the room. Students could follow this up by having an opportunity to create a future car that is compatible with their future fantasy.

4. Currently there is a new story emerging from groups such as holistic educators, environmentalists, and futurists. To help students identify this new story, have them search out resources that provide a positive futuristic view of a planet; one that has solved its problem with cars. Teachers may be able to use knowledgeable students as resources. Have students identify the values that are inherent in the future story and place these values on the Story Model diagram.

5. Have students examine *A Creation Story* in the Appendix to see how the values of the ideal story are also contained in the traditional stories of many cultures. One resource for traditional stories is *Keepers of the Earth* (Caduto & Bruchac, 1989).

6. Have students collaboratively generate a new story which realistically continues the *useful* from the old story and the *realistic values* of the ideal story. Have students maintain realism in the new story by reconciling the negative elements that seem to be inherent in the useful aspects of the old story. For example, the car has provided individual freedom at a major cost to the environment. As a starting point students may wish to diagram elements of the story as follows:

worst	new story	idea
no freedom of movement	a community transportation system that ...	personal freedom
O_2 tanks and gas masks		

7. Have students use the Story Model diagram to extract the probable and the ideal future stories and to assess these scenarios realistically to create a personal story. To do this, the students should use the diagram for the model and identify the values that are part of each story.

8. To assimilate the ideas of a future story, have students create a model of their bedroom or house to reflect future technology. Ideas might be generated from *The Futurist* (see Floyd, 1990).

9. Have students work in small groups to develop an "Action Plan" that will allow them to realize a new future story. A problem-solving strategy in which they determine the specific steps needed to achieve their visions might be considered. Creative problem strategies can be found in *Holistic Learning: A Teacher's Guide to Integrated Studies* (Miller, Cassie, & Drake, 1990). After considering this, the teacher might role-play an expert on the future with a pessimistic perspective (for example, "Everything in this universe dies. It is time for the planet to die").

   As the students give the details of their action plans, the teacher in-role gives them reasons why these plans are unachievable (for example, "Human beings will never agree to a car-pool — we are too private by nature").

   Students must find ways to deal with these challenges. Alternatively, specific students may be given the task of challenging their peers' action plans.

Students should work toward developing a consensus in envisioning an action plan that has the greatest degree of success. Encourage students to defend their action plans with actual or projected statistical data.

10. Incorporate group action plans into a class action plan.

11. Reflective journal activity:

   • What can I do as an individual?
   • What can we do as a class?
   • What could we do as a school?
   • What could we do as a community?

12. Student develops a personal action plan.

Objectives

- To consolidate the material that was learned and ensure a holistic understanding of the model.
- To understand that the complete story includes the past, present, and future of the car.
- To connect the story to students' past experience and future actions.

Suggested Activities

1. Have students tell the whole story (for example, old, present, new) in a "creative" way. Strategies could include:

   - creating a three-part mural or a triptych;
   - writing a child's history book from the future perspective;
   - writing a diary for someone who lived through each segment of the story;
   - creating an illustrated child's history book to show the segments of the story;
   - creating a storyboard of the past, present, and future stories; and
   - creating a tableaux or drama of some segments of the whole story.

2. Have the students tell the "whole" story of the car as it relates to them personally. Review their past, examine the present, and forecast how they will deal with the car of the future. (Students will have begun to reflect on personal future "stories" in previous activities.)

Action: Personalizing the Story

Objectives

- To connect one's personal story to the cultural story.
- To inform new ways of behaving.
- To prepare for the journey involved in behavior change.

Action

This last step is the final connection between the cultural and personal story. What is the student going to do to make the new story a reality? This stage involves personal exploration into the perceived past, present, and anticipated future. What values does the student live by? Are these the values that he or she wants to continue to hold?

Armed with a set of explicit values, the student can set goals to make these a reality. Creative problem solving can offer new solutions to old dilemmas. The personal story has been embedded in a new cultural story.

Suggested Activities

1. Review the "new story" that the class has collaboratively created to this point.

2. Have students make the new story explicit by using a guided imagery in which students relax and listen to the following to set a tone for telling stories about the imagined future. Provide students with these directions, in a quiet, soothing voice:

    "Focus your attention on your breath—relax, and every time you breathe out, let go of all the tension and tightness in your body. Imagine a warm, white light at the top of your head. As the light moves down through your body toward your feet, it warms and softens all the muscles in your body, just like a warm bath. The warm light is moving down through your face, over your eyes, through your cheeks, all the tension around your jaw melts as the warm light passes through it. Try to see in your mind the future story. Imagine where you work, what your home is like, how you get to work, the 'tools' you use to do your work."

    Have students quietly write down the things that they have visualized and share these through a class discussion. After developing sufficient information through the guided imagery, have students tell their future stories in pairs, then in groups of four. Each group of four may then generate a collaborative story which combines the common elements in the individual stories. These collaborative stories may then be presented to the class in a variety of ways:

    *   storytelling (one or more members of the group re-tells their story);
    *   enactment;
    *   readers' theatre (the story is scripted and given a dramatic reading);
    *   story theatre (one student reads the story while the other enacts it silently);
    *   tableaux (students create a series of frozen pictures); and
    *   story writing.

3. Have students commit to action based on the new (future) story they identify. This could take the form of a personal action plan (for example, "Now that you have identified this vision of the future, what is your plan for how to act on this vision?"). To formulate their action plans, students might write segments in a learning log in response to specific questions. Students could be asked to write about what they have learned, personal responses (thoughts, feelings) about the new learning, what they want to find out, and what they will do about this. An alternative activity may be to write a projected log for a day that would be very different because of the nature of their commitment to changed actions.

4. Have the students use a creative problem-solving strategy to chart their course in solving a personal problem that relates to the new story. The problem to be solved could be "How can I continue to act responsibly toward the environment when my peer group puts me down?" One strategy could be the Wallas's problem-solving model. This model involves:

- uncertainty/ambiguity;
- problem clarification;
- preparation/frameworking;
- incubation;
- alternative search;
- alternative selection/illumination; and
- verification.

Another creative problem-solving strategy is following the pattern of "The Quest" found on page 33. The student then becomes the hero of his or her own journey. Change involves pain and struggle. This model involves planning for the pain and struggle ahead.

Note: More detail on these creative problem-solving strategies can be found in Miller, Cassie, and Drake (1990).

5. Discuss: "Awareness or self-knowledge is the first step toward personal or behavioral change." Identify personal behaviors that are incongruent with the values of the new story. For example, certain individual rights that are an assumption in the North American cultural story may not be compatible with group rights. The individual may believe he or she has the right to smoke, bear arms, or consume natural resources within a personal context. However, in practice, these rights can infringe on the group rights resulting in second-hand smoke, increased killings, and environmental destruction. These behaviors may be role-played in scenarios created in small groups.

Group members can brainstorm alternate behaviors that reflect the values of the new story. Groups can then ritualize these new behaviors and perform these rituals using movement, chant, and music. As rituals involve words and gestures that bind meaning together for the group, they can be used as a reference point for individual change. Students will enjoy creating their own rituals. An example might be a "burning negative values" ceremony. Negative values and behaviors could be written on pieces of paper and group members officially burn their papers in a fireproof container to symbolize letting go of old values. Group members can then brainstorm for positive values and write affirmations of these. An example is "I am loving and kind in my relationships with others." Affirmations can be placed in another container and students randomly choose one that may guide future behavior.

The Technology Story

The purpose of this section is to extend the focus of car to the broader topic of technology. This section allows students several opportunities to pursue independent study, starting with the knowledge developed earlier in the unit.

Students should be reminded that technology itself is value-free. However, people assign values to technology when they use it in specific ways for specific purposes. Today it seems that North American culture is being driven by a "technological imperative." We are being driven by technological advances without realizing the positive and negative values that are inherent in this "tool." Exploration into technology then should follow the same guidelines as the previous section on "the car" and should be viewed as a very important part of the cultural story.

To explore the Story Model to its fullest extent teachers are recommended to follow the same general pattern offered in the unit on "the car." The transdisciplinary perspective can be facilitated by having students develop transdisciplinary webs. This would be particularly effective if different groups of students take a different technological focus, for example, computer, media effects, reproductive technologies. Groups could then compare the interconnections from different groups. Values embedded within the web should be explored at this point. The explicit values will probably be autonomy, independence, high standard of living, and so on. The implicit values will probably involve greed, power, consumerism, and manipulation.

Choose any of the activities from the car unit to elicit the values from the cultural story of technology. As well, a diagram of the Story Model should be posted on the board so that students can refer to it throughout the unit. Through this strategy, news items and world events can be connected daily as students bring them into class. The students should also be keeping a personal journal throughout the unit.

Suggested Activities

1. Explain the concept of a "ripple" effect to students (that is, the waves generated by a stone dropped in water) as a metaphor, to identify the influences that the discovery of a resource has on other aspects of a commu-

nity. For example, how does the discovery of the computer affect the population, employment, land use, and business viability?

2. Have students examine consumer trend charts for one or more current technological devices. Pose and answer questions about the technology.

3. Tell students a story about the development of one form of technology (for example, the computer), and have them pose several questions about the content of the story. Students can use their questions as the basis of independent inquiry.

4. Have students examine one or more biographies of Industrial Age laborers and have the students make a list of the characteristics of that person's life as identified in the biography. Students could undertake a systematic comparison of laborers from several ages. Alternatively, students can interview workers who have worked or are working in industrial factories today.

5. Have students examine old and new pictures of an industrial community such as Sudbury, and compare the characteristics of the community before and after pollution programs have been put into place. Students could also develop a more global perspective about pollution by examining other industrial centres around the world (for example, London, Mexico City, Tokyo).

6. Bring a technological device (for example, a pendulum clock) into the classroom and have students take it apart and/or repair it to examine how it works. Students may be interested in researching the various "inventions" that were required during its development.

7. Ask students the question, "When did the technological age start?" (Students may not all agree on an answer.) Then they examine different examples of technology. Ask, "How does change in technology affect our lives?" Discuss.

8. Have students examine the population statistics of some country such as Kuwait or Uganda and look at possible correlations between population fluctuations and the introduction of some form of technology. Resources such as the United Nations Yearbook or Stats Can may be used.

9. Have students examine any one institution in our culture (for example, theatre, medicine, photography, etc.). They can list, draw, and describe any of the technologies presently used in that institution. Students could start this exploration of one institution by developing a transdisciplinary map to record their brainstormed ideas. Choose a storytelling form to present this to the rest of the class.

10. Ask some professionals or "blue collar workers" or laborers into the classroom and allow students to interview these people in an effort to find out how

the jobs these people do have changed over the past decade or two as a result of technology.

11. Guide the students in imagining what their community might look like in the year 2050. Students should be reminded that there will be a past, present, and future at this time. Then, have students work in small groups of four or five students to tell a story from the point of view of either themselves or a selected character for each of the past, present, and future stories that students imagined. Students might need some reflection time prior to the storytelling to plan the specifics of their story. Teachers might group students for storytelling by having those students with a particular characteristic in their image of the community meet at a spot in the classroom where a sign has been posted to describe that characteristic (for example, "Sense of Futility in the Community").

12. Have students work in small groups to study the Industrial Revolution and then develop a role-playing scenario to have students examine its effects on people from various walks of life (for example, an industrialist, a child, a houseworker, a laborer — both union and non-union).

13. Have students prepare a consumer report on a new technology and generate a sales plan and a pollution control plan that is cost-effective for the technology.

14. Use Hypercard or another data base to store and manipulate data students have collected about their community. Have them generate a list of questions about another nearby community and arrange to swap data disks with a classroom in that community.

15. Have students complete the designing activity described below.

Materials: 12" x 18" newsprint
18" x 24" manilla paper
Paint and various sizes of brushes

- On 12" x 18" newsprint, students make realistic contour-line drawings of parts of a bicycle (for example, peddle, brake, handle, and so on) or another machine/device could be substituted (for example, musical instruments, sports equipment). All drawings should suggest how the parts work.

- On the 18" x 24" manilla, the realistic drawings are made into an abstract composition by:
  — Selecting a "focal point" on the manilla paper for the composition.
  — All lines, textures, and so on, should flow from or to this focal point.
  — Abstract the realistic drawings by redrawing them using: distortion of shapes, overlapping of shapes, enlarging shapes, and superimposing shapes.

- Outline in black using a half-inch brush.

- By using one secondary color and variations of it (for example, hues), paint the shapes leaving parts of the outline showing.

- Students should consider the harmony and balance of shape and color as they work.

- Action lines could be added later using white paint to emphasize movement of objects.

16. Have students create a Venn diagram and write one word on each circle of the diagram with "Technology" in one of them. Then pose the questions, "How do the other things overlap with technology?", "How do they overlap with each other?" Have students write the areas of overlap on the appropriate parts of the Venn diagram.

17. Have students write the story of their life journey. Review the past and the influence of technology in their lives. Then students project themselves into the future and imagine how they will deal with new technologies.

18. Have students use newspaper and magazine articles they have collected to put together a story of technology that is relevant to their new story.

19. Develop an action plan to fit the new story. This will involve a personal and class action plan. Students could develop contracts with each other where they will "coach" or "mentor" each other through personal change.

6
Assessment

Assessment at its best is a dynamic process involving individuals and groups reflecting upon the meaning that their learning experiences have had upon their lives.

Assessment should be: intricately related to the learning outcomes; reflect the image of the learner as an individual who is a capable, self-reliant, self-motivated lifelong learner who values learning as an empowering activity; and a shared responsibility between the teacher and the student.

On Determining Criteria for Assessment

In this book, we view education as an outcome-based assessment process. The focus is on acquiring skills for the productive citizen of the twenty-first century. We believe all students have the ability to acquire those skills if the curriculum is set in the context of personal relevance. However, the necessary skills may not be the same as the traditional skills that are presently valued. As a result, we discovered that determining the criteria for assessment was a very difficult process. When we looked to available resources we found that suggested evaluation strategies did not focus on what we had hoped to assess. Thus, we had to look at the Story Model and ask what it was we really wished to assess. We knew how to assess acquisitions of facts and certain skills. Yet, this curriculum was intended to engage the student at a personal level and increase the ability to make interconnections and the willingness to collaborate. As well, we wanted students to become aware of the implicit values inherent in the "content." Finally, the story model is intended to facilitate student self-direction and ability to manage change. We chose these as assessment criteria.

We suggest that assessors look beyond the traditional expectations to ask "What is it that we really wish to assess?" As well, they may wish to refer to the assessment documents listed in the references. Only then can suitable assessment strategies be put in place.

Criteria for Assessment

Within the context of this document, these are the suggested criteria for learning outcomes. Generally, the successful acquisition of these skills needs to be determined by performance-based assessment.

Criteria	Indicators
1. Personal Engagement	Does the student: • initiate activities? • show excitement during learning? • make personal comparisons? • go beyond classroom contexts to extend personal inquiry? • encourage involvement with others? • contribute to group discussions? • show evidence of reflection?
2. Ability to Make Connections	Does the student: • connect cause/effect relationships (for example, past to present or present to future stories)? • identify how focus (for example, car) can be extended to the theme (for example, technology)? • make connections among personal, cultural, and global stories? • connect ideas among disciplines by giving supportive arguments from various disciplines? • involve himself/herself in relaxation and visualization activities?
3. Change Management	Does the student: • show a tolerance for ambiguity during the change process? • manage change in a positive way? • encourage others to make change? • express the intention to change? • take positive risks? • recognize his/her progress toward positive change?
4. Self-Direction	Does the student: • generate questions/foci for inquiry? • form intentions to act? • make plans?

Criteria	Indicator
	• seek assistance and resources as necessary? • persevere through ambiguous situations? • use reflection to redirect and improve the learning process?
5. Willingness to Collaborate	Does the student: • develop a collective story? • share individual learning with others? • "piggy back" ideas in a group? • negotiate to arrive at shared meaning? • demonstrate individual accountability?
6. Awareness of Values in Story	Does the student: • recognize his/her personal story? • recognize the cultural/global story? • recognize how the cultural/global story shapes his/her personal story? • extract values from stories? • recognize both implicit/explicit values? • act on positive values?

Evaluation Strategies

We see these evaluation strategies as generic and applicable to all or many of the holistic learning strategies. Assessment of learning outcomes tends to be performance-based rather than a reliance on pencil and paper tests. Most of these assessment tools are qualitative by nature rather than quantitative and allow for the continual feedback to the student on his or her performance.

Observation
Observation is the key method of assessing student performance. We find out more by observing students in process than perhaps any other way. Rating scales, checklists, and participation charts can be tools for recording students' behaviors,

levels of achievement, or amount of progress. Much of observation can be recorded with qualitative data. A teacher's journal can be a procedure for teachers to maintain records. One example of record-keeping is for a teacher to record a behavioral description of what each student is doing at a certain moment in the class period (Suzie is writing, John is daydreaming). Over time, these observations will show a pattern.

Portfolio
A continuous file that provides a comprehensive summary of a student's accomplishments (for example, samples of work in various stages from first draft to completion, self-selected "best" work, and written reflections).

Teacher–Student Conferences or Interviews
These allow opportunities for the teacher and the student to share their expectations and evaluations of the learning experiences in order to establish future goals mutually. This is a collaborative review of performance.

Peer and Self-Evaluation
The skills for peer and self-evaluation take a long period of time to establish but they assist the student in seeing the role of evaluation as a tool for positive growth. Students need to be taught how to evaluate in a positive, but realistic, manner. Teachers can teach students observation techniques. Students feel more comfortable beginning peer- and self-evaluation by assessing group work processes rather than a product. The teacher should work from the large group evaluation to self-evaluation as the student shows readiness and comfort with the method. Starting with the group product and progressing over time to the self-evaluation of a student's own work should also be done.

A key issue here is the students' ability to understand and develop criteria for their peer- and self-evaluation. *Students need to be involved systematically in developing criteria.* Much of this depends on the readiness of the class and the individual for this step. Criteria must be explicit for all students but should be developed collaboratively. This process enables students to "step back" and look at their own development and growth with a responsible view.

Response Journals
Teachers can model by writing and then sharing their journals. Students will need guidance in reflection and finding their own voice. The teacher may consider the following when evaluating journal entries. Has the student:

- included a variety of personal responses?
- shown growth in positive attitudes over a period of time?
- formulated questions from their experiences?
- reflected on other's opinions, their own emotions?
- expressed a relationship between past and present learning?
- gone below the surface to ask "so what?" "now what?"
- evaluated his/her learning through the process of journal writing?

Graphic Representation

Can students understand and apply subject matter by translating information from texts, lectures, films, or experiments into graphic representations such as concept map or summary diagrams?

Independent Study Projects

Independent study projects determined by the student's interest can offer a rich source of data for assessment of higher order skills such as organization, synthesis, and interpretation.

In-Basket Simulation

An assessment strategy where the teacher poses a variety of problem-solving tasks that require on-the-spot analysis, synthesis, and evaluation by the students. The students can tell, write, or role-play what they would do and why.

A Final Note:

This is the end of our story. Now we are in the process of implementing the ideas that we have presented here. Each of us has tried these concepts in different settings and is convinced that they are powerful. May you enjoy adapting these ideas to your own setting. Perhaps you will also find that "a story is worth a thousand facts."

Good luck!

Appendix
Sample Narratives

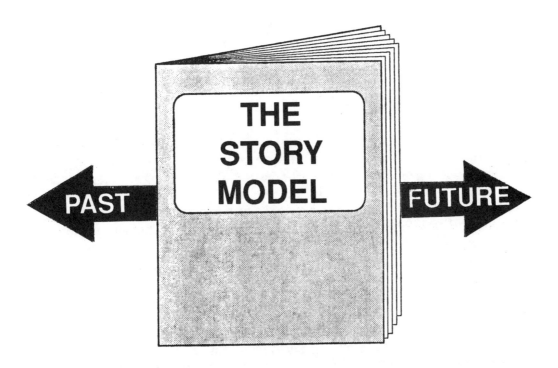

THE STORY MODEL

PAST ← → FUTURE

Henry Ford

My name is Henry Ford and I was born on a farm in Wayne County, Michigan, in the United States on July 30, 1863. This was two years before the American Civil War ended and only four years before Canadian Confederation.

When I was a boy, the United States was an agricultural country. But, unlike today, farm labor was mostly accomplished by hand. Few machines were available to make farm labor easier. As a young farm boy, I turned common events into experiments to satisfy my curiosity. At eleven, I tested the power of steam and blew up my mother's teapot in the process! Sometimes, however, my experiments were helpful. I constructed a water wheel to turn the household coffee grinder when I was only twelve years old. By the time I was fifteen, I was well known in my community for my ability to repair watches. At sixteen, I left the farm to learn a machinist's trade.

However, I did not forget the hard-working farmers of my boyhood! Only four years after leaving home, I had built a steam-powered "farm locomotive," a pioneering version of today's tractor. The destruction of my mother's teapot hadn't been in vain! I finished my machinist's apprenticeship in 1883 and started work for Westinghouse. There, I set up and repaired steam engines.

From 1891 to 1899, I worked for the Edison Illuminating Company of Detroit. I was chief engineer in the light bulb producing company from 1893 to 1899. While working for Thomas Edison's company, I continued my own experiments with engines.

In 1893, I built a one-cylinder gasoline-powered engine in my kitchen. The cylinder is the hole in the engine that has the piston travelling up and down in it.

Later, I used old steam exhaust pipes to make hand-made cylinders which were then mounted on four bicycle wheels. I drove this vehicle even after dark, with light provided by a kerosene lamp. At 4:00 a.m. on June 4, 1896, I drove my invention, a "car," around the block from my home. The noisy invention was released from my kitchen by the removal of part of the house's brick wall!

This first "car," or quadricycle, had a top speed of only 25 miles per hour (40.2 km/h) and no reverse gear or brakes. During the next four years, I worked to improve on this design. In 1899, I left the Edison Illuminating Company to become chief engineer of the Detroit Automobile Company. Soon, I found that my ideas were very different from those of my new employer. The Detroit Automobile Company tried to produce a small number of automobiles for the very wealthy. I dreamed of greater things. I wanted "... a motor car for the great multitude ... so low in price that no man making a good salary (would) be unable to own one."

I knew the value of strong publicity to sell my motor car to large numbers of people. To gain publicity, I built and raced several cars. In 1904, I set a world record for the mile in 39-2/5 seconds (about 23 sec/km), racing on the winter ice of Lake St. Clair in the famous "999."

In June of 1903, I started the Ford Motor Company which became an investor's dream. I started the company with $28 000 that was provided by twelve investors. One of the investors put up only $100 and sold her shares only seventeen years later for $260 000! Nine of the twelve investors became multimillionaires. In 1919, my son Edsel and I became sole owners of the company by purchasing shares for seventy-five million dollars. The Ford Motor Company made my dream of mass production a reality. In 1903, 1708 Ford cars were built and sold. By 1927, after eighteen years of production, the popular Model T Ford had been produced fifteen million times.

Mass production became possible in the Ford Motor Company by using a moving assembly line. Early in 1913, the company was producing the flywheel magneto, a car engine part, on a moving assembly line. By the middle of the same year, car frames were also being produced on an assembly line. I retired and turned over the leadership of the Ford Motor Company to my son Edsel in 1919. Edsel Ford ran the company for twenty-four years until his death in 1943. As a retired entrepreneur, I again led the company until 1945 when my grandson, Henry Ford II, became president of the company.

* * * * * * * * *

Henry Ford died in his home near Dearborn, Michigan, on April 7, 1947. In honor of his many achievements, a museum in Greenfield Village, in Dearborn, Michigan, houses one of the most complete collections of vehicles in the world, including Henry Ford's first automobile.

Thomas Berry

(Thomas Berry is an ecologian living in the United States. This story is adapted from a talk he gave in Toronto, Ontario.)

I grew up in the foothills of the Appalachian mountains in North Carolina. I was born in 1914, and the natural world was still somewhat unspoiled. It was beautiful. As a child I had access to woodlands, meadows, and creeks. One of my most vivid memories is seeing the Eastern Bluebirds. They would sit on posts. Then they would begin migration in late February or early March. They became flashes of brilliant blue in the sky. This was the way I grew up.

At the time I was reading boys' outdoor magazines and had the idea that the Northwest was the only natural part of the world left. It was kind of a sacred direction for me ... and I wrote for catalogues with canoes and camping equipment in them. I had plans for my life that included surviving in the wilderness.

But this was the early 1920s. The automobile was just coming into existence. The roads were just being paved. Life was beginning to be mechanized. By the time I was about eight or nine, I already had a sense of things being destroyed. I hated the automobile from the first time I saw one. I saw it as an enemy. Why? Because I liked to walk and run barefoot and I liked to ride a bicycle and this bothered me.

I always remember in the early days when they had the Ford, the Model T. It was open and when the rain would come, people would put the window pieces on the side to keep the rain out. Then the rolled up window was invented. I always remember loving to be out in the rain; I loved to be out in the summer rain and get soaked. I would see people inside these automobiles with these rolled up windows and marvel how silly these people were. How could they be so protected from such a great experience? What happened?

The Blacksmith's Story

It was Mr Ford's factory that killed things for me. When his Model T's began rolling off the assembly line, people went crazy for them. Soon the wagons and buggies lay idle, or folk around here tried to sell them for scrap and kindling so they could make the down payment on one of those infernal machines. It was only the few farmers left on the land who came in for their horses to be shoed, or to have the odd harvester repaired.

And then my two young apprentices left to work in Mr Ford's factory. Better pay, they told me. No "old man" ordering them around any more. Besides, they said, there was no future in fixing buggies. So now there will be no one left to learn the skills I learned from my father, and that he learned from his.

The foreman came by and offered me a job at the plant, operating one of the big presses that punch out metal for the doors. "Come down and try it out for a while," he said. And so I did, but when I saw the men on the assembly line, doing the same job over and over no better than machines, I knew I wouldn't last a week. "Where else are you going to find work?" they asked me. "Who's going to need a blacksmith now?"

So I'm thinking of loading my tools and anvil on my wagon, and heading west, where the new settlers are beginning to farm. I hear the roads there aren't any good for automobiles, and besides, the foreigners won't have the money to buy them for a long while yet. And maybe one of the younger ones would want to learn an honest trade.

A Retired Man

Oh, I hear you about the environment and I KNOW I shouldn't drive my car so many places. Yes, I hear you when you tell me I'm destroying the ozone layer — and yes, it is terrible that almost all the men over sixty in Australia have skin cancer because of the depletion of the ozone. Oh yes, I feel kind of guilty about driving my car unnecessarily but I'm an old man now. Your mom and I like to putter around now I'm retired — it's what we do for entertainment. I've worked hard all my life, paid my taxes, paid my dues ... I've looked forward to this time ... I don't know how much longer I've got really and, I'm sorry, I'm not going to stop driving my car .... I've usually used your mother's little car ... that's something at least. Anyway don't keep on about the environment. You don't understand. We can't just stop consuming. We need jobs — that's the most important thing. If we didn't have jobs, people wouldn't survive ... and if we don't produce consumer goods, we wouldn't have jobs... so it's not as easy as you claim .... Anyway, humans have probably been on this planet long enough. It's probably time to end the planet ... so I might as well enjoy the time I have left driving my car.

Production Line Worker

Working on the assembly line at General Motors in Oshawa can be a very boring job. Day after day for eight hours a day, I bolt doors onto car bodies with an air-driven wrench. From Monday to Friday my job remains unchanged. When I started working here you didn't need a grade 12 education, but now all the new workers do.

Robotics have taken over some of the more boring jobs, but my job still remains repetitive and boring. Sometimes I just hate to come to work. Often my co-workers are absent from their jobs on the line.

The job has its good points. If I work overtime or on the weekend, I get paid two times the normal hourly rate. Every six months, at 10 percent below the market price, we are allowed to buy new cars made by the company. We're highly unionized and we strongly support our local branch. Thanks to our union we have very good health and medical benefits.

Although the job can be boring, I don't take work home to be completed like an office worker or teacher, and our extended benefits are at least the equal of other higher-paying jobs. As well, I can often read whatever I want while working on the line. There's a lot of shut-down time, and besides, I don't need much concentration to do what I do.

Life in a Car Town

I, Michael Moore, was born in Flint, Michigan. As a child I was happy, healthy, and lived the life of a well-adjusted kid, thanks to the General Motors plant. General Motors made everyone in Flint happy and prosperous when I was a kid. Everyone in my family worked for G.M. My parents always seemed happy working for General Motors. The car was the symbol of prosperity and happiness for all.

Then Roger Smith, chairman of General Motors, closed down our plant in Flint. My life changed. My parents, along with 38 000 others in Flint, lost their jobs because of the G.M. shutdown.

It was reported that the rat population now surpasses the people population by 50 000 due to people leaving Flint and the budget constraints on the city's garbage collection. The police said Flint had the highest crime rate in America due to unemployment. The town erected a five-storey jail house to try and stay on top of the crime wave.

Unemployment caused many families to be evicted. The unemployed tried to make a new life for their families by leaving Flint. Things changed radically. Those who kept their jobs lived very, very well. Flint became the unemployment capital of the country. Families couldn't pay their mortgage or rent and were forced to leave their residences. Many left town.

My life used to be happy. The car plant was our "savior." Now what do I do? Where do I go? I don't want to become a criminal or get evicted.

The car sure did change my life.

(Adapted from the movie "Roger and Me.")

The Legend of Gaia

I am Gaia, Mother Earth. I live. I breathe. I am all powerful in my scope and splendor. Since the beginning of life, three and one-half billion years ago, I have had the power to regulate and replenish my resources. Millions of organisms live upon my body and are dependent upon me to sustain and nourish their lives. Within my body every organism is linked. Microbes, plants, and mammals, soil dwellers and ocean swimmers, are all caught up in the constant cycling of energy and nutrients from sun, water, air, and earth. This global exchange system flows through my veins by way of various transport mechanisms, from ocean currents to climate patterns and winds. I regulate and regenerate myself through the exchange of gases, the travels of animals, and the processes of feeding, growth, and decay. Throughout my total life zone, change and diversity, specialization and interdependence, are found at every level.

Once I was strong, powerful, and omnipotent. But now I, Gaia, am weak and ill. My once rich and lustrous skin is now dry, sallow, and flaking. The daily encroachment of creeping deserts and the loss of nutrients through erosion are taking their toll on a body that was once overflowing with fertility and the potential for life. More and more, my life-giving flesh is ploughed under and covered over to make way for the foul-breathing metal shells which criss-cross my body. My insides are being ripped apart daily as humans recklessly mine the richness of the elements within me, in order to create the tools by which they can control each other.

My crowning vibrant mane which once shone like an emerald in the sun is now patchy and fading, due to the shrinking of my forests. Acid rain and the dumping of chemicals into lakes and rivers have clogged my veins and arteries, blocking the delivery of valuable nutrients to my body. The deterioration of the ozone layer and the 450 000 tons of lead released into the atmosphere each year pollutes my air. This disruption of the natural interchange of gases leaves me wheezing and gasping for breath.

My bodily fluids, the oceans, where life first began more than three-and-a-half billion years ago, were once teeming with an abundance of resources that I, Gaia, could draw upon. Now, the oceans receive the brunt of human waste and are slowly being destroyed through over-harvesting and the destruction of natural habitats.

The organisms which inhabit my body are fragmented and fiercely competitive. Their desire for dominance and the increasing violence which they heap upon each other in order to achieve it, not only bring about irreparable damage, but also consume resources at an intolerable rate.

I, Gaia, cry out in pain. Who will listen? Who will share my pain and suffering? Who will help me to restore the fragile balance upon which my life depends?

The thunder of my anguish, the swirling winds of my despair, the chaotic turbulence of my body's temperature, and the foul air with which I breathe will unleash upon humans a desperate cry for help. Who will hear? Who will see? Who will help me?

A Creation Story

When the world was very new, the Creator gave all people the things that they needed to be happy. Although everyone had food and lots of land, two brothers began to argue over the land. Each gathered support for his claims, and war appeared to be unavoidable.

One night when the brothers slept, the Creator carried them to a new place on what is now the northwest coast of North America. When they awoke, the brothers found themselves in a beautiful river valley surrounded by mountains that stretched high into the clouds. This river is now called the Columbia.

The Creator gave each of them a bow and one arrow and told each of them to shoot the arrows into the air, and when each arrow landed, the brother who owned that arrow would become a great chief in that land. Each brother took his followers to their new lands. The Creator constructed a great stone bridge across the river which divided their lush lands.

For years, the two groups lived in peace moving freely back and forth across the bridge, but eventually they became envious of each other. The Creator grew angry and darkened the sky and took away their fire, leaving them cold in the autumn and winter.

They cried and prayed for fire to ease their suffering and promised to live in peace with each other. The Creator took pity on them and went to the lodge of the old woman Loo-Wit, the only source of fire on the earth.

Loo-Wit, who had not been greedy, had avoided the anger of the Creator, and now the Creator promised her anything if she would share her fire with the people of the two brothers.

Loo-Wit said, "I want to be young and beautiful."

"You shall be," said the Creator. "Take your fire to the middle of the stone bridge and share it with all the people. Keep it burning at all times to remind people that their hearts must be good."

As the sun rose through the darkness, people saw the young and beautiful Loo-Wit on the stone bridge and came to get fire and stop their quarrelling. Once more their homes were warm and peaceful.

Unfortunately the two brothers both noticed how beautiful Loo-Wit was, and each desired her for himself. The two brothers once more began to quarrel and their people joined in the quarrel. The Creator had enough of this and changed each brother into a mountain. One mountain, on one side of the river, is now known as Mount Adams. The other mountain on the opposite side of the river, is now called Mount Hood, but even as mountains they continued to quarrel, throwing fire and stone at each other, narrowing the Columbia River at a place called The Dalles.

Loo-Wit was heartbroken to think that her beauty had caused so much trouble, and she longed for peace. The Creator took pity on her and changed her into the most beautiful of mountains between Mount Adams and Mount Hood. Loo-Wit was allowed to keep the fire and slept peacefully as Mount St. Helens.

Although she sleeps, people today are aware that she was placed between two quarrelling mountains to keep the peace. Her beauty was intended to be looked upon and admired and to remind people to share the land and keep it well. People have said that Loo-Wit will again awaken and let everyone know how unhappy she and the Creator are if they do not respect the land.

T's Journey

T set off from the familiar coast she had known so well. There was little she could do now but look ahead into the unknown, for her old life was becoming a distant memory. It was with great hope that she entered upon her journey, yet she knew that there would be many obstacles to overcome if she was to gain the wisdom she would need to become the best teacher she could be.

At first the weather was fair. The brisk, but steady, wind carried her at a comfortable and constant clip. Then, on the more distant islands where she stopped to refresh her supplies of food and drink, she began to hear tales of a land where a fearsome monster, half human, half beast, stood in the way of the teacher who sought the ultimate goal. Fear entered her heart, but she knew in her bones that there was no going back, that it was only in moving ahead in her journey that she could achieve success.

The weather became tempestuous. The wind and waves lashed her little boat, threatening it with destruction. T knelt, and grasping the gunwales to keep herself from being swept away, she took three steadying breaths. She imagined herself in an ideal classroom, one in which all of her students were creating and sharing their stories, learning from and supporting each other, and enthusiastically and actively involved in discovering what they needed to know in order to complete their own journeys.

A flash of lightning branded this vision into her mind. Thunder rolled across the sky, and a monstrous wave washed over and capsized the boat, flinging T into the watery chaos. Summoning all of her remaining strength, she swam toward what appeared to be a rocky shoreline.

****

When T awoke, a boy stood over her. He spoke no words, but pointed to a building in the distance. T followed the boy as he led her there.

As they approached the building, T realized that it was a school. The boy led her into a classroom. The students were working in groups of three around the room, and when T entered with the boy, they all stopped what they were doing and approached her. Then one of the students spoke.

"Listen carefully," she said. "Soon you will enter the cave of the Beast. There will be great danger there, but with strong will and an open heart, you will achieve your goal." "The Beast is terrifying," said a boy beside her, "but if you follow our instructions, you will surely succeed."

"Take an amulet," said a third student who moved toward her from the back of the group. "When the Beast sees you, hold it to your heart and visualize my face. Stay beyond the grasp of the Beast and enter the back of the cave. There you will see a door. Enter the room, and you will find what you need."

T looked at the girl, letting her image impress itself upon her mind. She held out her hand, and as soon as T touched the amulet, the girl disappeared. The room faded into a dark, swirling mist. A foul, noxious smell filled the air. T knew she was in the cave of the Beast.

Staying close to the wall of the cave, T made her way forward. The smell became stronger. Clasping the amulet, she recalled the wondrous classroom she had imagined when she was on the boat. She knew that if her vision was to become reality, she would have to find her way to the back of the cave. She had no choice now but to move ahead.

The Beast roared as it became aware of her presence. It came right at her, its knife-like claws thrashing outwards to slash its prey. T's first impulse was to run, but summoning all of her courage, she pressed the amulet to her heart and visualized the girl's face. A soft, barely audible voice seemed to speak within her, saying that now she would be safe. T felt as though she was being enveloped in a warm, golden light that emanated from her chest and filled the cave. The Beast reclined against the wall, pacified and whimpering.

T moved carefully past the Beast. When she came to the back of the cave she was surprised to find three doors. Which one would she choose?

Then she knew what she had to do. She grasped the amulet and held it to her heart, and as she did so, the middle door began to open. Without fear, she entered.

To her amazement, she found herself in the staff room of the school at which she worked. It was just as she left it — teachers talking and drinking coffee, phones ringing in the adjoining office. Had it all been a dream, she wondered?

But there, around her neck, was the amulet. Looking up, T saw that there was a paper in her (third from the end) mailbox. When she took it out, she noticed a photograph in the corner — it was a photograph of the students she had met on the island! Underneath was a note:

Dear T,

Congratulations! You have faced the Beast and have returned unscathed. Your students are waiting. They have many gifts to offer you. As you did with us, listen to them and take them into your heart and mind, and they will help you set your course.

There are many resources that will aid you, but only those that help your students develop the confidence to risk their own journeys should be trusted. Watch and listen to your students, then decide.

Your journey is not over, but only just begun. Trust yourself.

From all of us.

The bell rang, and T walked down the hall toward her classroom, the amulet glowing warmly near her heart.

Barton, B. (1986). *Tell me another*. Markham, Ont.: Pembroke Publishing.

Barton, B., & Booth, D. (1990). *Stories in the classroom*. Markham, Ont.: Heinemann.

Berry, T. (1988). *The dream of the earth*. San Francisco: Sierra Club.

Caduto, M., & Bruchac, J. (1989). *Keepers of the earth*. Saskatoon: Fifth House Publishing.

Drake, S. (1992). A novel way to integrate curriculum: The Story Model. *Orbit*, *23* (2), 5-7.

Drake, S. (1991). How our team dissolved the boundaries. *Educational Leadership, 49* (2), 20-22.

Drake, S. (1991, Fall). Journey of the learner: Personal and universal story. *The Educational Forum, 56*, 47-59.

Egan, K. (1986). *Teaching as storytelling*. Chicago: University of Chicago Press.

Feinstein, D., & Krippner, S. (1988). *Personal mythology*. Los Angeles: Jeremy P. Tarcher.

Floyd, T.H. (1990, Nov./Dec.). Personalizing public transportation. *The Futurist*.

Gardner, H. (1983). *Frames of mind*. New York: Basic Books.

Hargreaves, A., & Earl, L. (1990). *Rights of passage*. Toronto: Ontario Ministry of Education.

Hesford, W. (1990 Fall). Storytelling and the dynamics of feminist teaching. *Feminist Teacher*, 20-24.

Miller, J. (1988). *Holistic curriculum*. Toronto: OISE Press.

Miller, J., Cassie, B., & Drake S. (1990). *Holistic Learning: A teacher's guide to integrated studies*. Toronto: OISE Press.

Murdock, M. (1987). *Spinning inward*. Boston, MA: Shambhala.

Pike, G., & Shelby, D. (1988). *Global teacher, global learner*. Toronto: Hodder & Stoughton.

Scull, K. (1992). A holistic approach to teaching history. *Orbit, 23* (2), 14-15.

Values, influences and peers (1984). Toronto: Ministry of Education.

Further Recommended Readings

Allender, G. (1991). *Guided imagery and education*. New York: Praeger.

Andrews, B., Gardner, J., & Hubbard, K. (1983). *Student evaluation: The bottom line: A teacher's guide to student evaluation*. Toronto: Ontario Secondary School Teachers' Federation.

Baker, A., & Green, E. (1987). *Storytelling: Art and technique* (2nd ed.). New York: Bowker.

Bauer C. (1977). *Handbook for storytelling*. Chicago: American Library Association.

Brady, M. (1989). *What's worth teaching: Selecting, organizing and integrating knowledge.* New York: SUNY Press.

Breneman, L., & Breneman, B. (1983). *Once upon a time: A storytelling handbook.* Chicago: Nelson Hall.

Caine, R.N., & Caine, G. (1991). *Making connections: Teaching and the human brain.* Alexandria, VA: Association for Supervision and Curriculum Development.

Cook E. (1969). *The ordinary and the fabulous: An introduction to myths, legends, and fairy tales for teachers and storytellers.* New York: Cambridge Press.

Cornfiels, R.J.; Coyle, K.; Durrant, B.; McCutcheon, K.; Pollard, J.; & Stratton, W. (1987). *Making the grade.* Scarborough: Prentice Hall.

Educational leadership: Integrating the curriculum (1991, October), *49* (2).

Eisler, R. (1987). *The chalice and the blade: Our history, our future.* San Francisco: HarperSanFrancisco.

Eisler, R., & Loye, D. (1990). *The partnership way: New tools for living and learning, healing our families, our communities, and our world.* San Francisco: HarperSanFrancisco.

Etobicoke Board of Education (1985). *Making the grade: Evaluating student progress.* Scarborough: Prentice-Hall Canada Inc.

Etobicoke Board of Education (1988). *Evaluation of the language arts in the intermediate division: Grades 7-10.* Toronto.

Fogarty, R. (1991). *The mindful school: How to integrate the curriculum.* Pallatine, Il: Skylight Publishers.

Galyean, B. (1984). *Mindsight.* Berkeley, CA: Center for Integrated Learning.

Gibbons, M. (1991). *Slashing a pathway to education 2000: Self-direction, integration, challenge graduation.* Bowen Island, BC: Personal Power Press.

Hamilton, M., & Weiss, M. (1987). *Children tell stories: A guide for teachers.* Burke, VA: Tandem Publishers.

Holistic Education Review, 39 Pearl Street, Brandon, VT. 05733-1007, (809) 247-8312.

Jacobs, H. H. (1989). *Interdisciplinary curriculum design and implementation.* Alexandria, VA: Association for Supervision and Curriculum Development.

Kovalik, S. (1991). *Teachers make the difference - With integrated thematic instruction.* Village of Oak Creek, AZ: Books for Educators.

Lazear, D. (1991). *Seven ways of knowing.* Pallantine, Il: Skyline Publishers.

Lincoln County School Board (in press). *Growing collaboratively: Breaking the barriers, dissolving bridges.* Toronto: Prentice Hall.

Metropolitan Toronto School Board (1989). *Together we learn: Cooperative small group learning with a focus on the intermediate division.* Toronto.

Metropolitan Toronto School Board (1990). *Does this count?: Evaluating achievement in the transition and the specialization years: A resource handbook for administrators.* Toronto.

Miller, J., & Drake, S.M. (Eds.). (1992, May) . Holistic education in practice. *Orbit* (Special Issue).

Ministry of Education (1990). *Assessing language arts.* Toronto: O.A.I.P.

National Council of Teachers of Mathematics (1991). *Mathematics Assessment.* Reston, VA: The National Council of Teachers of Mathematics.

Parsons, L. (1990). *Response journals.* Markham, Ont.: Pembroke Publishing Ltd.

Perrone, V. (1991). *Expanding student assessment.* Alexandria, VA: Association for Supervision and Curriculum Development.

Saskatchewan Education (1988). *Understanding the common essential learnings: A handbook for teachers*. Saskatoon, Sask.

Spady, W, & Marshall, K. (1991, October). Beyond traditional outcome-based education. *Educational Leadership 49,* 67-72.

Tchudi, S. (1991). *Travels across the curriculum: Models for interdisciplinary learning*. Richmond Hill, Ont.: Scholastic.

The Green Teacher, 95 Robert St., Toronto, Ontario, M5S 2K5, (416) 960-1244.

Toronto Board of Education (1980). *Observing adolescents in their developing years*. Toronto: Board of Education.

Toronto Board of Education (1980). *Observating children through their formative years*. Toronto: Toronto Board of Education.

ABOUT THE AUTHORS

Susan M. Drake teaches at the Faculty of Education at Brock University, St. Catharines, Ontario. She is the author (with John P. Miller and J. R. Bruce Cassie) of *Holistic Learning: A Teacher's Guide to Integrated Study* (OISE Press, 1990).

John Bebbington is an elementary teacher with the Scarborough Board of Education. His areas of expertise include social and environmental studies, history, and geography.

Sander Laksman is with the London Board of Education, Ontario. He is currently a vice-principal of an elementary school.

Pat Mackie is a vice principal of a junior/middle school in Etobicoke, Ontario. She teaches part-time at Brock University in research in social environmental studies.

Nancy Maynes is Director of the Ontario Thinking Skills Consortium. She is a part-time instructor for Nipissing University in their principals' courses and for Brock University in their pre-service program.

Larry Wayne is an education consultant with the Waterloo County Board of Education. He specializes in English language arts and drama.